The International Design Yearbook 20

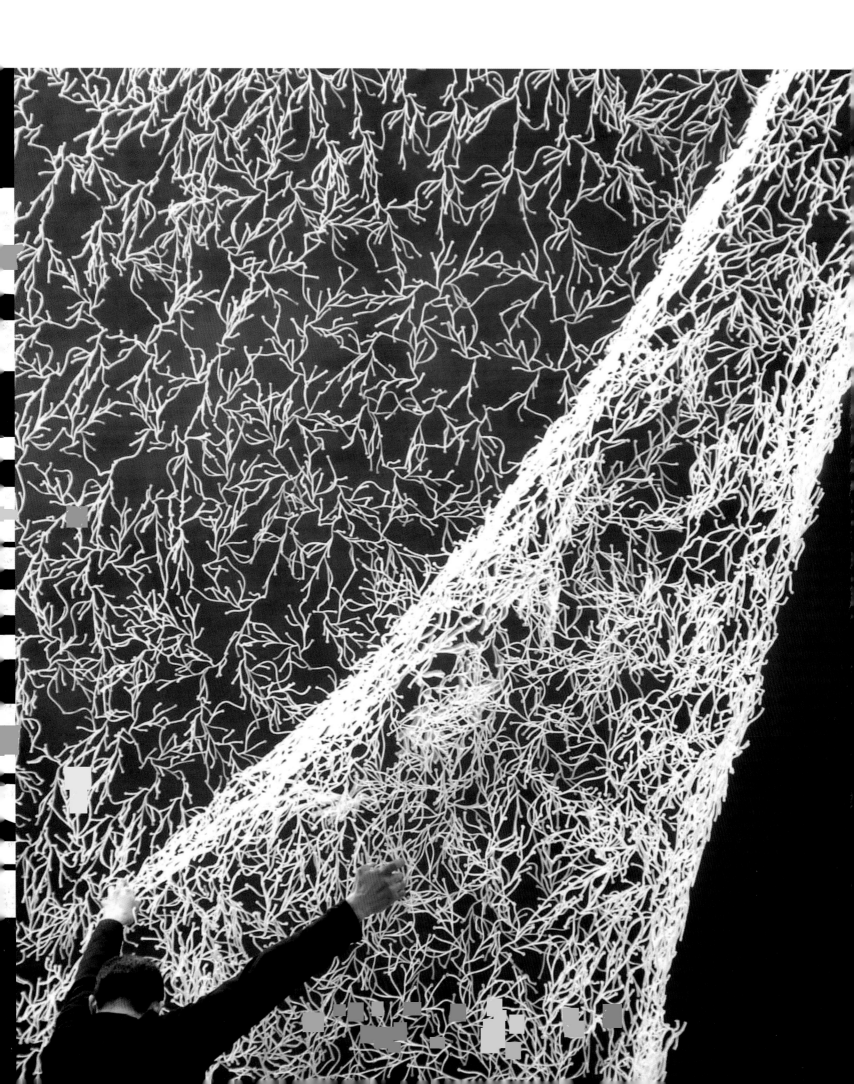

The International Design Yearbook 20

Edited by Marcel Wanders

Abbeville Press Publishers · New York London

Based on an original idea by Stuart Durant

Guest Editor: Marcel Wanders
General Editor: Jennifer Hudson
Designer: Roger Fawcett-Tang, Struktur Design
Project Manager: Anne McDowall
Assistant Editor: Fredrika Lokholm

First published in the United States in 2005 by Abbeville Press
137 Varick Street, 5th Floor, New York, NY 10013

First published in Great Britain in 2005 by Laurence King Publishing
71 Great Russell Street, London WC1B 3BP

ISBN 0-7892-0852-0

Printed in Singapore

First Edition

10 9 8 7 6 5 4 3 2 1

Library of Congress Cataloging-in-Publication Data
available upon request

For bulk and premium sales and for text adoption procedures, write
to Customer Service Manager, Abbeville Press, 137 Varick Street,
5th Floor, New York, NY 10013 or call 1-800-ARTBOOK.

Front jacket images:
Chair, Nic, by Werner Aisslinger
(see page 42)
Surface pattern, 72 daisy red,
by Debbie Jane Buchan
(see page 67)

Back jacket images:
Speciality cutlery, Style, by Daniel Eltner
(see pages 160–161)
Printed fabric, Saskia, by Manuel Canovas
(see pages 196–197)

Previous page: 'Algue' modular clipping
system by Ronan and Erwan Bouroullec
(see pages 138–139)

Contents

Foreword by Marcel Wanders

Grow more fish

Gijs Bakker used to tell me that designers don't read. That makes me feel good and helps me overcome my fear of the blank page as I write this foreword. What can I say to an audience of design professionals? Why do we need a design yearbook? That was the first question that popped into my mind after being asked if I would like to edit *The International Design Yearbook 2005*. Is it important to evaluate and discuss quality? Do we need to make a document that will review the year? Is it for our children, or for our parents, so that they can show it to the neighbours and be proud of us?

I believe in design. I believe design is one of the great things man can do for the benefit of the community in which he is living. I believe we need 'progress' because we want to feel meaningful, and, beyond that, to feel alive. Life is about change, and if we create new things, then we contribute to the certainty of life. If the life I live is inspiring to others, I live a meaningful life.

If there's a single reason why design is so important to me, it is probably the potential it gives me to inspire, to contribute to the concept of a world changing in the direction my heart and head want to go. This is my primary focus as I work and play around in the garden of our industry. If we want to become an inspiration to others, we have to become communicators. Scream if you want to be heard!

We have to grow out of our own little world, to find new people to speak to and new people to listen to. We have to make as many crossovers as possible. Secure in our little box, we can become too comfortable and fall asleep. We all agree with each other too much. It's sometimes scary to see that what we consider to be a great piece has no meaning at all to a wider public. May this book be a welcoming invitation to people outside our design field and an encouragement to us on our trip outside the box.

We all fish the same pond, and today – in a challenging business environment – we are perhaps inclined to try to steal fish from our neighbours instead of growing them ourselves. This is where I see the great purpose of this book: I hope it will be an ambassador that will inspire us all to grow more fish. I am happy that the publisher, Laurence King, who has created this yearbook for the past 20 years, has agreed to make a contribution to this cause by sending a copy of the book to 100 people in different fields, each of whom has a great influence on modern life. I want to inspire them – and many others – with our activity, our spirit, the ideas from our hearts and our vision for the future.

But more importantly – and possibly more effectively – I want to ask you to help me. When you have finished reading – and hopefully enjoying – this book, please do not lay it aside on your valued bookcase. Instead, hand it to a person you feel you can inspire with these little pictures, these little pieces of writing, these little signs of passion for creating a new world.

Be an ambassador and create more fish!
Grow more fish – fish will eat.

a TALE OF
CHILDREN
aND
BaTHWaTER

a FABLE by
MaRcel WaNDeRS
with pictures by
SHANNON McNeiLL

KNOTTED CHAIR
1996

ONCE UPON a time in a VERY small coUNTRY, FAR away FROM here, THeRe LiVeD a BaKeR who PRepaReD his bread with mUCH love and gReat care.

CaREFULLY he kneaded his dough and baked His bread. He worked FROM morning till NiGHT, always aiming FOR THe Highest quality and paying attention to the smallest detail. He baked all kinds of bread, and made sure that his BReaD had a daRK, crispy crust.

As the baker always said:

FLOWER table
2001

"BREAD withoUT a crust is like a house withoUT a ROOF."

But, people complained to the baker about his bread all the time. One person got the crust stuck between his teeth, another one's gums started to bleed. For the older people or those who were sick, the crust had to be taken off. To make things worse, someone cut his hand when the knife slipped off the hard crust. To FORCE the CHILDREN, who were RELUCTANT to EAT the BREAD, parents told them THEY WOULD ONLY LEARN to WHISTLE if THEY WOULD ALSO EAT THE CRUST.

Splinter
2001

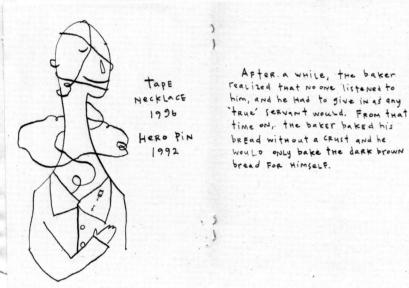

Tape
Necklace
1996

Hero Pin
1992

After a while, the baker realized that no one listened to him, and he had to give in as any 'true' servant would. From that time on, the baker baked his bread without a crust and he would only bake the dark brown bread for himself.

round light
1998

His clients were delighted with the new, modern bread, and they were proud of their baker's innovations. They were no longer bothered by bleeding gums or tough crusts. It was easy to cut the bread and pleasant to eat for children or toothless older people.

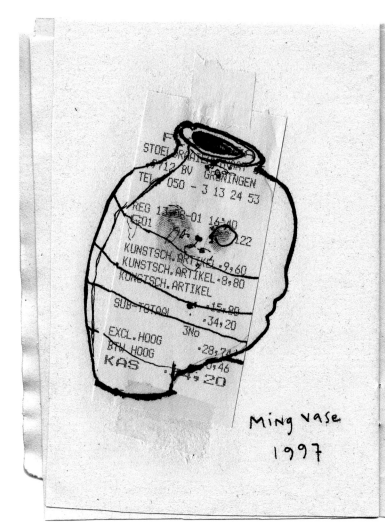

Ming vase
1997

The village was happy and a long time passed by until, one day, a young lad on his way to the field was captivated by a strange and beautiful sound. He looked around to see where it came from and found himself in front of a bakery. He saw the baker blow a cheerful tune and heard the baker's wife follow its rhythm with a knife while ticking crosses onto the bread.

The boy, who was barely nine years old, was completely flabbergasted by this spectacle. Blowing through his rounded lips, he hurried home where he asked his mother to explain what had happened. His mother explained that blowing like that was called "whistling" and that this had not been done for a long, long time. You had to eat the crust of the bread to learn to whistle, and that was no longer the custom. She told her son that at breakfast, someone usually ended up with a crust between his teeth and would remind them of the mishap for the rest of the day. And she told him how her own mother used to cut off the crusts of her bread when she had been sick in bed, and how important that had made her feel.

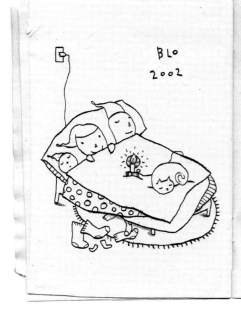

BLO
2002

The boy, who felta bit uncom-
fortable about his mother being
so touched, hurried back to the
baker to order that mysterious
bread with the crust. Several
people in the village noticed
this, and within a short period
of time, the entire village
talked about it. The people
remembered the bread with the
crust and how nice it was.
Soon the village was bothered a-
gain by children who whistled,
sick people who did not want
crusts on their bread, by bleeding gums, and by crusts stuck
between the teeth.

sponge vase
1997

And the baker?

Carefully he kneaded his
dough, and, aiming for the best
quality and taking care of
every detail he worked from
early in the morning til late
at night.

And the village?

Happily it ate bread with a
crust forever and ever after.

the
End

by Jennifer Hudson

Introduction

For the past 20 years, *The International Design Yearbook* has been documenting the trends, styles, personalities and prevailing dogmas of domestic design. Nineteen internationally renowned, and very different, designers and architects (Robert Stern, Emilio Ambasz, Philippe Starck – Guest Editor of both the 1987 and 1997 editions, Arato Isozaki, Oscar Tusquets Blanca, Mario Bellini, Andree Putman, Borek Sipek, Ron Arad, Jean Nouvel, Alessandro Mendini, Richard Sapper, Jasper Morrison, Ingo Maurer, Michele De Lucchi, Ross Lovegrove, Karim Rashid, Tom Dixon and now Marcel Wanders) have added their personal interpretations. And so each issue has not only recorded what's new, characteristic, thought provoking, inspirational, distinctive, memorable, weird and witty, but has provided an insight into the many and varied approaches these respected individuals take towards their work, how they evaluate the output of others and what they expect (or not) from design generally.

The *Yearbook* was born at a time when the design world was maturing from post-Memphis excesses and settling into a significant creative trend. Liberated from the strictures of Modernism, there was a renewed enthusiasm for objects that took their influences from the past, from their physical

'Can of Gold', produced continuously since 2001, is a social-action initiative as well as a designed product.

context and from culture itself. The orthodoxies of different design schools were, for the moment, overturned, and individuality and experimentation ruled. It was an exciting time to be involved in design, and the need to record such a zeitgeist was the driving force to produce a tool to document this renaissance.

Our 'diary of design', has continued to offer an invaluable insight, as well as a comparison of work from its respective periods. A comprehensive record of complex trends, innovation, and of evolution and decline, the volumes provide a kaleidoscopic journey through two decades of design.

From the mid-'80s to the mid-'90s, a progression can be traced, from the free spirit of the post-Modernist revolution to Minimalism, which came as a reaction to this self-obsession; the recession of the '90s, where comfort, commercial viability and function outweighed the desire to innovate; and on to the rise of 'moral design', which was green, energy-efficient, environmentally friendly and questioned consumerism. At this time Starck was writing 'we have everything we need and too much we don't need. We're entering a more moral market where people like me, whose responsibility is to produce, must ask themselves about the legitimacy of their work.'

By the end of the '90s the books record an innovation in product design rather than furnishings. New materials and techniques led to sub-miniaturization of computing technology. The forms of computers and accessories were small and friendly and no longer dictated by their function. Computer chips could even be printed on paper substrates that meant a newspaper could become a computer, connected by incorporated radio and satellite to the whole globe. Information science and communications media were beginning to transform design.

The volumes since the millennium have witnessed a liberating pluralism, and this edition is no exception: a state of affairs I predict will continue for a while to come. For the past five years, the design community has been in a state of flux, where no one style or trend has dominated. There has been a slow breaking down of the barriers between disciplines, cultures, roles and skills: this is an era in which there is a place for craft-based, low-tech, individualistic approaches as well as mass-produced high tech. Despite an unhealthy economic climate, this lack of a specific direction, harnessed to the absence of a specific design protocol, has led to an increase in experimentation and the rise of conceptual design – design as communication, interactive objects, products that could be considered 'too close to the art gallery' (Tom Dixon) for comfort, but which, nonetheless, aim to re-define our perception of design and stimulate international discussion.

Any technological innovation is largely hidden. Advanced production methods and the growing use of CAD programs to develop objects has led to research into the use of new, more pliant materials that can be moulded into the softened and rounded shapes created by these digitalized programs. This ISDN revolution has led to a greater sophistication of products and has accelerated not only the speed of the manufacturing process but also of change itself. The computerized production chain that originally resulted in the destruction of individuality can now be customized to allow designs to be manipulated and personalized: a sophisticated 'smart' industrial process, which allows for individualism on a commercial, mechanized scale.

In the 2003 *Yearbook*, Karim Rashid talks of 'desk-top manufacturing', which he believes is just around the corner and will allow the consumer to build up a three-dimensional object using a stereolithography machine, or alternatively personalize a product by engaging with a visual program on the Internet. These designs could then be transferred to the manufacturer's site, produced and delivered. Karim and his vision of 'design for all' nicely introduces two trends that have grown steadily over the last five years and that have been illustrated and discussed time and again within the pages of recent *Yearbooks*: namely, the increased democratization of design and the rise of the design personality.

Throughout the '60s and '70s retailers such as Habitat and IKEA succeeded in bringing affordable contemporary design to the masses, yet it took the design press a little while to catch on. With big names such as Arad, Starck, Rashid, Dixon, Alessi and Swatch taking design from the showcase

'Airborne Snotty Vases' (2001), inspired by the existent yet non-visual shapes of human sneezes.

and on to the high street, the majority of fashion magazines and leading newspapers began to include dedicated life-style sections. Specialized press religiously covers the latest trends, no matter how tenuous they may be, and more perniciously has made celebrities out of a few. The media society is a lot to blame for building up personalities only to knock them down again. It's a dangerous development, as there is a plethora of products that today are conceived to look good in the design magazines, and designers who will be forever tied down to a period or nailed to a style. As early as 1997, Starck was writing: 'the media are forever creating and destroying images of people. What the designer has to understand is that honest and passionate work creates its own consensus – a consensus that takes longer than the timetable of the media – and it is that consensus, that time which supports and nourishes the true designer.'

For a designer to last the vagaries of time, he needs to beat the press. By approaching his work in a broader context, by looking at civilization and society and by thinking of semantics as well as aesthetics, he will be able to make the transition from the moving sands of the media to the solid ground of peer recognition and posterity.

Marcel Wanders is one such. That's not to say that he isn't loved by the design press. Tall, handsome, flamboyant, loquacious, mischievous, confrontational, passionate, mercurial, opinionated and uncontrollable, he has enough of the showman about him to guarantee saturation coverage not only in The Netherlands but also internationally. Yet Alex Wiltshire summed him up perfectly in his article for *Icon* magazine in April 2004 when he wrote: 'Marcel Wanders is an inventive and highly original designer, but at the same time a theatrical marketing man and a practical business man with a conscience'.

Today it is not enough for designers to just design. Because of the press hype and the competitiveness of celebrity, there is a tendency for them to become prophets with a missionary zeal to preach. Wanders certainly has that fanaticism, but he is as interested in how the world can change him as in how he can change the world. Wanders learns from the past and seeks to build up dialogues with his consumers. To make a product successful, he is convinced there needs to be two committed parties: the designer with the message and the recipient, who needs to be open and aware.

When I first met Marcel during the Milan Furniture Fair 2003, it was with a view to sounding him out as a possible future Guest Editor for *The Yearbook*. Immediately striking was his utter dedication to what he does and his passion to contribute something to make the world a better place, to create objects that mean something in everyday life. He looks on his works as narratives: 'For me, designing revolves around this idea, around the fact that what I make means something to other people, around the notion that a design communicates.' For this reason, the objects and interiors he produces do not alienate. They are timeless and classical yet innovative and surprising. As he likes to say: 'My designs are

The 'Stone House' workspace for the Dutch insurance company Interpolis in Tilburg (2003).

humorous but never a joke.' He likes to stretch archetypes to the limit, to invent the unexpected, but never slips into parody.

When we spoke on that occasion, his conversation revolved around his belief that today the West is too preoccupied with invention and doesn't value enough the lessons it has learned from the past. He believes that there are too many designers trying too hard to invent the new – products that may have an appeal for a season or two but that in the end have a built-in obsolescence, as 'nothing ages so quickly as something that looks too new'. Wanders is strongly of the opinion that the consumer likes variety but needs security. We like to be surprised, but we want to feel comfortable with the objects we choose to fill our environment.

In the end, designs have to be commercial, and it's this balance between the innovative and the saleable that informs much of his work and ensures his continuing success. It's also the lack of saleability that he blames for the crisis in Dutch design at the moment, and is one of the reasons he founded Moooi in 2001. Because of the generous state subsidies given to designers in The Netherlands and the creative freedom taught in its design schools, Dutch design is strong conceptually. It has influenced the way we look at design because it has redefined imperfection and material qualities and has developed an industrial process in a craft environment. But it has yet to develop a way of translating this commercially.

Wanders' design collaborative, Moooi, is the first step in addressing this imbalance. In control of both the design and the manufacturing process, it provides the opportunity to reconsider artistic aesthetics and produce products in a realistic and industrial way. The company has also instigated a training programme to encourage younger designers to make objects that can be mass-produced while retaining a unique appearance. Marcel says: 'I want Moooi to be a business. I think that so many designers run their companies like artistic free places. I think in the end it won't grow, it won't reach a lot of people because it's an academic enterprise, where it's more done for the designers than the people.'

Marcel's personal inventiveness lies in the way he manipulates materials (especially natural substances) and techniques, as well as the standard aesthetics we associate with certain objects. He recycles ideas and archetypes and reinvents the ordinary, but produces designs that would not seem out of place in anyone's front room. From the iconic 'Knotted Chair' onwards, nothing is quite what it appears. Here, a hand-knotted net of rope has been coated in epoxy resin – what appears soft is hard. Similarly, the 'Crochet Coffee Table' he designed for Moooi in 2002 has a look that belies its materiality. The 'BLO lamp' may seem to be Wee Willie Winkie's candlestick, but clever technology allows this electric light to be extinguished when blown on. The 'Airborne Snotty Vases' could be random sculptures, but in fact were formed by recording sneezes in a scanner and translating these patterns into the finished item via a CAD program and an SLD machine. The 'Can of Gold' is not just a designed item but an act of social activism. Conceived to celebrate the first anniversary of Galerie Xpressions, a small venue for young artists in Hamburg, Marcel found a way of linking the art world, the consumer and the local homeless. The gallery purchased 100 tins of soup, the contents were distributed and the cans were then washed, gilded, distinctively labelled and sold. The proceeds generated enough capital for the local welfare institution to re-invest the following year for the benefit of the homeless. Marcel sees the concept being taken up by different cities, each sealing the product with their individual labels to create an international philanthropic series of precious containers. To date three further cities have taken part. More recently, the 'Carbon Chair', which he designed with Bertjan Pot, may look substantial, yet it is 'as light as the line you need to draw it on paper', and the interiors of the 'Stone House' workspace in the Tilburg headquarters of the Dutch insurance company, Interpolis, question the alienating and now antiquated idea of the standard office by housing communal areas – meeting room, dining area and chill-out zones – in cave-like structures, while keeping the work-stations in the open areas alongside.

Wanders is not a person who likes to have constraints put upon him, or to consider that anything is impossible. Whether working on a specific object (who else can transform a sneeze into a thing of beauty), an interior design project (there aren't many who could conceive, let alone create, mannequins that actually breathe as Wanders managed to do for the Mandarina Duck flagship store in London) or on any undertaking, no matter how small, he will push the edges of the envelope. It's this enthusiasm he brought to the selection of *The Yearbook*. He is not always the easiest person to work with because he demands perfection in whatever he does, but the end result (as with this book) is worth the battles to get things just right. Again talking to Alex Wiltshire for *Icon*, he was quoted as saying 'I can do anything. I could have been a dentist and I would have been the best dentist ever ... I'm

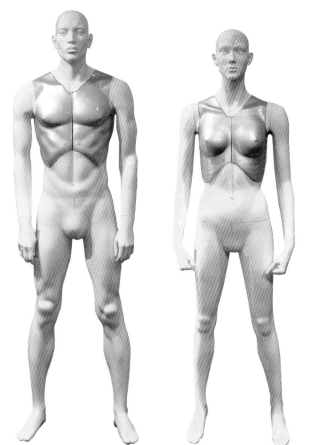

Mannequins that 'breathe' for the Mandarina Duck flagship store in London (2001).

pretty sure that whatever I'd have done I'd have done it with so much passion and love that I'd do a great job... If I feel challenged ... I can come up with good solutions.'

The pages that follow bear witness to this dedication, in the breadth of designs selected, the way in which the book is ordered and the introduction of some interesting new features. With the same philosophy he adopts for his designs, Marcel wanted to create a dialogue with the consumer. Instead of theming the items selected into categories, he wanted to present a seamless progression of objects that share a similar dynamic, whether of type, material, colour or shape. In order that these products should not be seen in isolation, he has composed a list of design highlights from the last year, events that help to put the work illustrated in context (see pages 230–1). To enforce his message that design is part of a greater whole, and with the aim of inspiring people outside the design world to collaborate with designers in the future, Marcel has also requested that copies of the book be distributed to key players in the fields of art, architecture, theatre, business, graphic design, fashion, the culinary arts, dance, interior design and art direction. And so that his voice should not be the only one heard in these pages, he has invited a number of colleagues to add their personal comments on some of the objects illustrated. I hope you enjoy the book as much as I enjoyed helping to put it together.

Product   Handheld vacuum cleaner, SG67
Designer   Stefano Giovannoni
Materials   Stainless steel 18/10, thermoplastic resin
Dimensions   H: 14 x W: 11.5 x L: 38.5cm (5 ½ x 4 ½ x 15 ⅜in)
Manufacturer Alessi SpA, Italy
Website   www.alessi.com

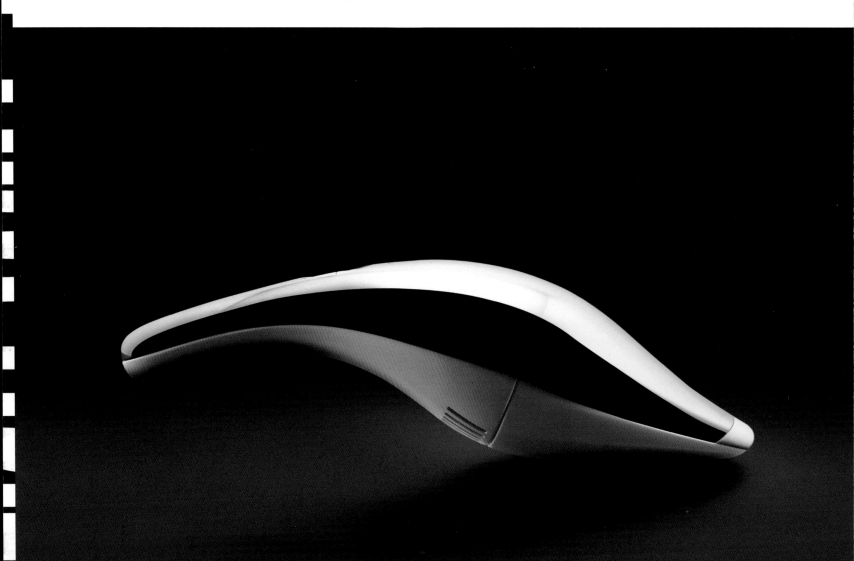

Product	Double pitcher, Mix drinks
Designer	Guido Metz & Michael Kindler, Metz und Kindler Design
Materials	Glass
Dimensions	H: 19.5 x W: 13.5 x D:21.3cm (7 ⅞ x 5 ⅜ x 8 ¼in)
Manufacturer	WMF Aktiengesellschaft, Germany
Website	www.metz-kindler.de

A perfect example of form following function, Metz and Kindler's tableware collection for WMF has just what is necessary with no extraneous detailing. 'Mix Drinks' is simply two jugs that fit together, one for water and the other for the juice or wine to be diluted. Like the samovars of the orient, 'Opera' (see page 59) is a big pot with water and a little can with the tea-extract: the kettle acts as a warmer and the can as the teapot. The coffee system 'More Kult' (see page 109) consists of a chunky espresso coffee maker, milk jug, coffee container with integral spoon and the first mechanical milk foamer. By pressing ten times, enough force is created to make the perfect cappucino.

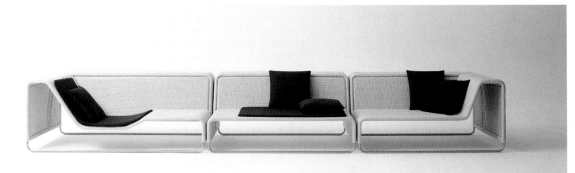

Product	Modular sofa for outdoor environments, Island	Product	Carpet, Mat
Designer	Francesco Rota	Designer	Paola Lenti
Materials	Stainless steel, cover in synthetic 'Rope' fabric	Materials	'Rope' synthetic yarn
Dimensions	D: 98cm (38 ½in)	Dimensions	W: (max) 200cm (79in)
Manufacturer	Paola Lenti srl, Italy	Manufacturer	Paola Lenti srl, Italy
Website	www.paolalenti.it	Website	www.paolalenti.it

Blurring the distinction between interior and exterior, Paola Lenti has developed a textile that can be used both inside and out. The modified polyolefin-based yarn, which is then twisted to create 'Rope', is reminiscent of the cords used by mountaineers and sailors. It is resistant to seawater, chlorine and sunlight, is non-permeable, non-allergenic and anti-mildew, and was engineered in collaboration with one of Italy's leading producers of high-performance yarns. 'Rope' can be woven and tufted to create different effects for various applications. Francesco Rota's series of furniture was designed specifically for this innovative material. The textile can also be hand-woven directly onto the structure of the furniture using a specialized traditional technique and takes the form of the piece onto which it is applied. The end result brings the qualities of comfort and elegance associated with an interior collection to exterior environments.

Product	Wall panel self-supporting system equipped with shelves and storage units, Eleven Five
Designer	Bruno Fattorini
Materials	MDF
Dimensions	Various sizes
Manufacturer	MDF Italia, Italy
Website	www.mdfitalia.it

Product	Set of cutlery, London
Designer	David Mellor
Materials	Stainless steel
Dimensions	(Table knife) W: 2.1 x L: 22 x D: 0.6mm (¾ x 8 ⅝ x ¼in)
Manufacturer	David Mellor Design Ltd, UK

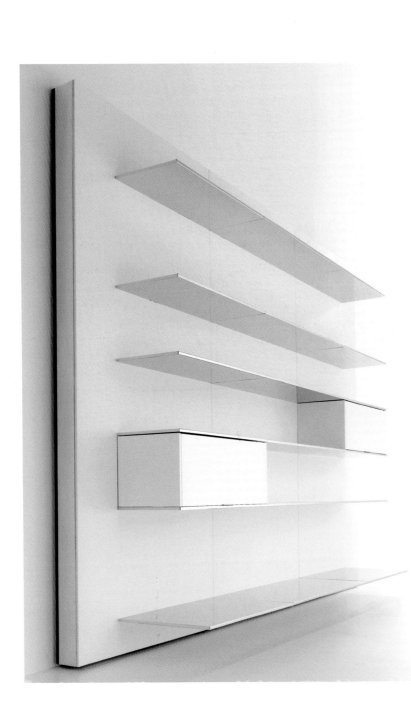

1

6

2

7

3

8

4

5

Product	Chair, Archaeology of the Invisible Collection
Designer	Maxine Naylor and Ralph Ball
Manufacturer	One-off, Studio Ball, UK
Website	www.studioball.co.uk

Product	(1) Day by Day
Materials	Polypropylene, steel
Dimensions	H: 80 x W: 50 x D: 65cm (31 x 19 ⅝ x 25 ⅝in)

Product	(2) Black Stack
Materials	Polypropylene, steel
Dimensions	H: 75 x W: 50 x D: 50cm (29 ½ x 19 ⅝ x 19 ⅝in)

Product	(3) Same Difference
Materials	Polypropylene, steel
Dimensions	H: 75 x W: 50 x L: 300cm (29 ½ x 19 ⅝ x 118in)

Product	(4) Co Dependant
Materials	Polypropylene, cast resin, steel, plaster
Dimensions	H: 80 x W: 55 x D: 55cm (31 x 21 ⅝ x 21 ⅝in)

Product	(5) Poly Propagation
Materials	Polypropylene, steel
Dimensions	H: 75 x W: 50 x L: 140cm (29 ½ x 19 ⅝ x 55in)

Product	(6) Starbase
Materials	Steel, aluminium, plastic, foam, vinyl
Dimensions	H: 100 x W: 70 x D: 70cm (39 x 27 ½ x 27 ½in)

Product	(7) 24 Star
Materials	Steel, aluminium, plastics, foam, fabric
Dimensions	H: 130 x W: 110 x D: 110cm (51 x 43 x 43in)

Product	(8) Plastic Gold
Materials	Polypropylene, gold leaf
Dimensions	H: 80 x W: 55 x D: 55cm (31 x 21 ⅝ x 21 ⅝in)

Working on the premise that items we come in contact with every day are never properly valued, Ralph Ball and Nadine Taylor have taken several chair archetypes and formed them into a series of set pieces that explore the implicit generics of chair culture and typology. Whether their starting point is the leg of an office chair or the way stacking chairs fit together, they look for new ways of expressing details or concepts within the object itself. The series is entitled 'Archaeology of the Invisible' and is from their 'Sustaining Desire' research project.

Product   Rug, Aros
Designer   Nani Marquina
Materials   100% wool
Dimensions   Diam: 100/200cm (39/79in)
Manufacturer   Nanimarquina, Spain
Website   www.nanimarquina.com

Product	Coffee table, Lo-rez-dolores table
Designer	Ron Arad
Materials	Corian, fibre optics, mirror, media
Dimensions	H: 40 x Diam: 160cm (15¾ x 63in)
Manufacturer	Limited batch production, The Gallery Mourmans, The Netherlands
Website	www.ronarad.com

Arad is internationally known for his unorthodox use of materials and his own unique style language, and his collaboration with DuPont Corian at the Milan Furniture Fair 2004 did not disappoint. Over the last five years Corian has found favour within the design community. Once thought of only as the expensive option, this blend of mineral and pure acrylic polymer is now frequently chosen for its unabashed man-made quality, its warmth to the touch and its malleability, which renders it suitable for the complex design shapes now being produced by CAD programs. The 'Lo-res-dolores-tabula-rasa' installation at the Gallery Gio'Marconi in Milan is the result of Arad's research into the creative possibilities of working with Corian. Going beyond Corian's practical uses, Arad wanted to experiment with, and exploit, the translucency of the material, bringing large sheets of blank white Corian to sudden life with film, music and images. Designed in collaboration with the Belgium-based company Barco, specialists in imaging technology and visualization, 'Lo-rez-dolores' is a lens-shaped coffee table into which 22,000 fibre-optic pixels have been embedded. The table shows moving images and issues sounds from the user's choice of media, but when switched off, the table is once again a smooth seamless white orb. Most plasma screens are black and unwelcoming when not in use; with Corian the 'screen' is a beautiful object in itself.

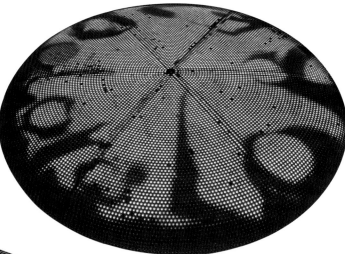

Product	Fabric, Tempura	Product	Fabric, Cincinatti
Designer	Design-Team nya nordiska	Designer	Design-Team nya nordiska
Materials	60% cotton, 40% polyester	Materials	70% polyester, 30% lurex
Dimensions	W: 140cm (55in)	Dimensions	W: 160cm (63in)
Manufacturer	nya nordiska textiles GmbH, Germany	Manufacturer	nya nordiska textiles GmbH, Germany
Website	www.nya.com	Website	www.nya.com

Product   Flowerpot, Suniside
Designer   Marc Krusin
Materials   Vicenza stone
Dimensions   H: 24 x Diam: 36cm (9 ½ x 14 ⅛in)
Manufacturer Klay, Italy

Product	Lamp, Zipper 40
Designer	Setsuo Kitaoka
Materials	Plastic zipper element, cloth ribbon,
	fluorescent lamps
Dimensions	H: 14cm (5 ½in)
Manufacturer	Corp. Modular works, Japan

With inimitable Japanese styling, Kitaoka Setsuo has twisted a 17-metre (58-foot) translucent plastic zip 40 times around a fluorescent tube to create poetry from the banal.

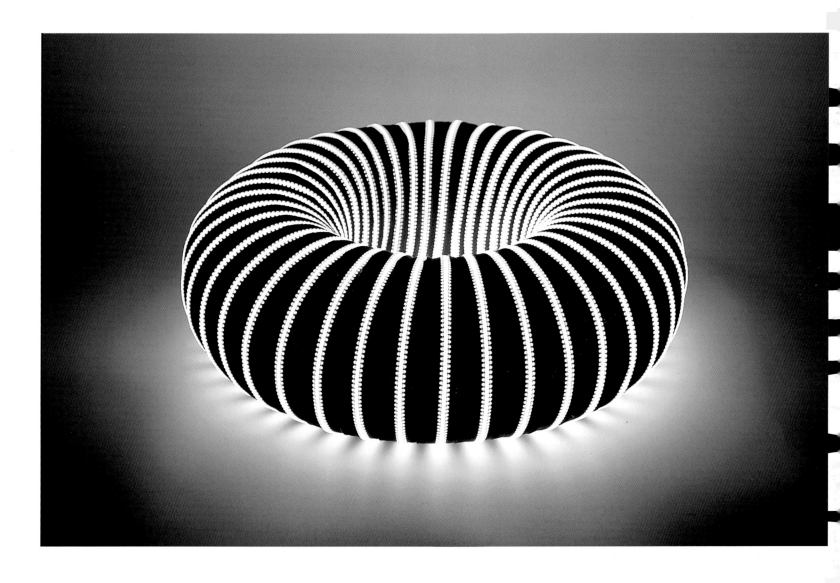

Product	Children's furniture, Happy Horse
	(Black Beauties Collection)
Designer	Ineke Hans
Materials	Recycled plastic
Dimensions	H: 60 x W: 28.5 x D: 52.5cm (23 ⅝ x 11 ⅜ x 20 ⅞in)
Manufacturer	Limited Batch Production, Ineke Hans/Arnhem,
	The Netherlands
Website	www.inekehans.com

'Black Beauties' is the latest of Ineke Hans' exploration of products in black, previous ranges that used this colour as their central theme being Black Gold (porcelain) and Black Magic (chairs). Ineke Hans trained in Arnhem, and then at the Royal College of Art in London. She worked for Habitat for three years before forming her own studio, returning to Arnhem in 1998. Her work is hard to categorize: it is design, yet it has sculptural qualities and relies heavily on collective consciousness and psychology, its appeal largely generated by the powerful effect her products have on our imagination and behaviour. Basing her work on recognizable archetypes, she subtly shifts our preconceptions and associations, throwing us off balance by experimenting with materials, narrative, existing codes and colour. In her book *Black Bazaar: Design Dilemmas*, which she wrote in collaboration with the journalist Ed van Hinte, she explores the various connotations of the colour black, from the negative – occult (black magic), associations of evil and 'otherness', death and racism – to the more positive – black as the colour for the style conscious, sartorial elegance (black-tie event) and luxury (ebony). By playing with codes, we form our opinions and make our judgements. No colour is just a colour, especially black.

Product   Stencil
Designer   Karim Rashid
Materials   Acrylic
Dimensions   W: 20.3 x L: 30.5cm (8 x 12in)
Manufacturer   One-off, Bozart, USA
Website   www.karimrashid.com

Product   Smart roadster & roadster-coupé
Designer   Hartmut Sinkwitz
Materials   Steel, alloy, plastic
Dimensions   L: 343 x W: 162 x H: 119cm (135 x 64 x 47in)
Manufacturer Smart GmbH, Germany
Website   www.smart.com

Walking in the streets of any European capital during the last year, it was extremely hard to miss the two nifty design additions to the automobile industry: the aluminium flash of the Davin spinning wheel (see page 190) and the small, but perfectly formed, Smart Roadster.

Handy as the Smart car is, there was always something rather embarrassing about actually turning up anywhere in one. But the Roadster is another matter. With the engineering might of Mercedes–Benz behind it, it goes without saying that it is extremely well engineered and made out of high-quality material, but more importantly for the design aficionado, it has already become a fashion object. Hugging the road, its muscular outline has nothing of the Noddy car about it and its low-cost, low-consumption stimulation is also just right for today's speed restrictions, traffic congestion and environmental pressures. The Smart Roadster comes in two models: the hard-top and the soft-top coupé, which share two design features that have elevated the sports version from the rather clumsy outline of its predecessor: namely, the normal-looking bonnet and four wheels the same size. Although it's difficult to climb into the Roadster, once there the fun of the ride is worth the effort. Sitting only inches from the road, everything around towers above you, and the proximity to the road gives a feeling of speed even though it's not the most powerful compact on the market. The French novelist and pilot Antoine de Saint-Exupery wrote 'A designer knows that he has achieved perfection not when there is nothing left to add, but when there is nothing left to take away', which pretty much sums up the Smart Roadster.

Product	Portable meeting room, Office in a Bucket
Designer	Nick Crosbie
Materials	Rip-stop nylon, PVC
Dimensions	H: 220 x W: 300 x L: 400cm (87 x 118 x 158in)
Manufacturer	Limited batch production, Inflate Design Ltd, UK
Website	www.inflate.co.uk

To write that Inflate have moved on since the mid '90s – when every major design magazine featured their range of inflatable tableware and lighting products – would be to underestimate the freshness, fun, practicality and affordability of these witty pieces. Yet, it is undeniable that over recent years their expanding product ranges and investigations into various manufacturing techniques have reached a maturity that has resulted in some very interesting items. 'Memo', in collaboration with Ron Arad, the 'S2' range in Corian and, most recently, what Nick Crosbie refers to as the 'Big Structures' all bear witness to this development.

The 'OIAB' (office in a bucket) is a progression of Inflate's forays into exhibition design and temporary inflatable spaces. Describing the concept of 'OIAB', Nick writes, 'Any idiot can set it up. If you know how to use a bucket then you should be able to use this'. For an inflatable temporary office space to work it has to be simple to set up and durable enough to remain sound after many uses. It also needs to afford a degree of privacy and tranquillity, while not being overly claustrophobic or taking up excessive storage space when deflated. To keep a sense of openness, Crosbie has removed the roof, making the outer walls curve. From outside, the space is enclosed, but from within, there is a 'skylight', which also eliminates the need for integral lighting. There is no door: the design opens and closes like a clam. Easily assembled, the whole 'room' fits inside a bucket with a fan at the bottom. The structure is connected to its container and self-inflates.

Product   Stackable Lounge chair, Orchid
Designer   Christian Flindt
Materials   Fibreglass, white glossy gel-coat finish
Dimensions   H: 81 x L: 130 x W: 115cm (32 x 51 x 45in)
Manufacturer Prototype, Christian Flindt, Denmark
Website   www.flindtdesign.dk

Product   Biscuit, Finger biscuit
Designer   Paolo Ulian
Materials   Biscuit
Dimensions   H: 3 x Diam: 3cm (1 ⅛ x 1 ⅛in)
Manufacturer   Limited batch production, Paolo Ulian Office, Italy

Product   Kitchen system, K11
Designer   Norbert Wangen
Materials   Stainless steel
Dimensions   Various sizes
Manufacturer   Boffi SpA, Italy
Website   www.boffi.com

in my studio we have
a specific someone :
who is always finger-
dipping the chocklade
jar, this is a great
invention for the peace
in my studio
M.

Product   Hand-printed wallpaper, Euro Dam
Designer   Paul Simmons, Timorous Beasties
Materials   Paper, ink
Dimensions   W: 52cm (20 ⅓in) (51.5cm / 20 ¼in repeat)
Manufacturer   Limited batch production, Timorous Beasties, UK
Website   www.timorousbeasties.com

By taking silhouettes of various European countries, mutating them into traditional damask patterns and adding screens to resemble the mountain ranges on relief maps, Timorous Beasties have succeeded – fortuitously or not – in producing a designer version of the psychoanalytical Rorschach Ink Blot test. In this wallpaper, not only beauty but also comprehension is in the eye of the beholder.

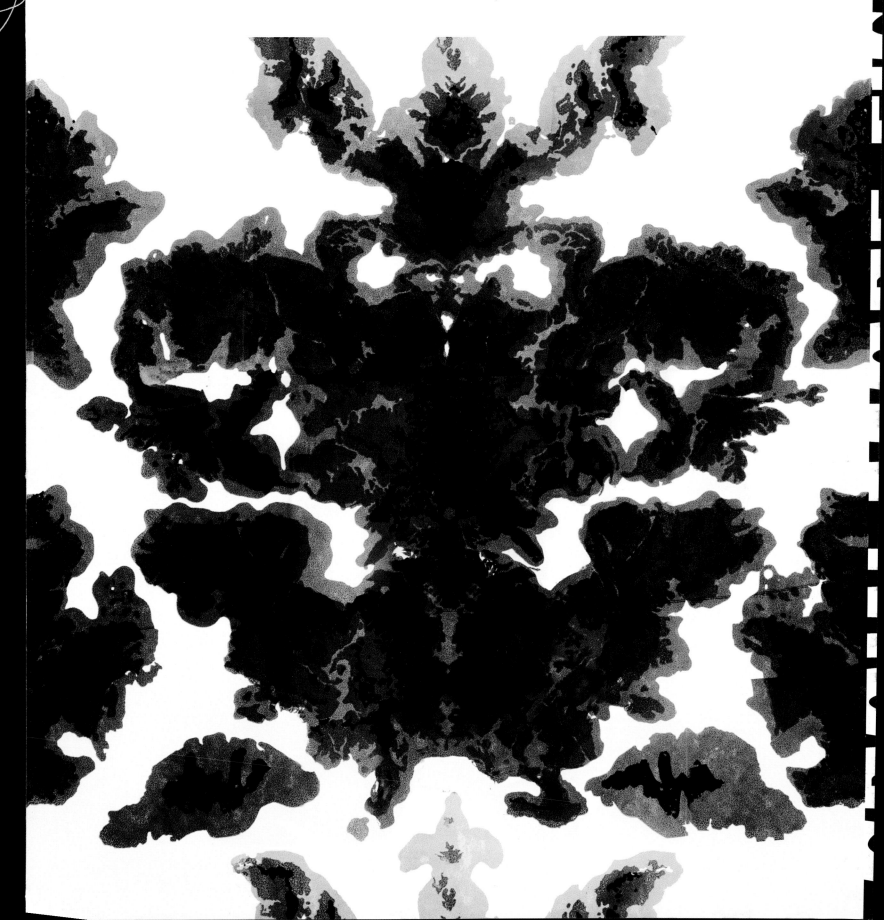

Product   Boxes, Custodie Collection
Designer   Giuseppe Rivadossi
Materials   Walnut
Dimensions   Various sizes
Manufacturer Limited edition, Numa/Serafino Zani, Italy
Website   www.serafinozani.it

Product	Suspension lamp, Fringe		Product	Rug, Estambul (Black on White Collection)
Designer	Edward Van Vliet		Designer	Javier Mariscal
Materials	PVC/cotton laminate on metal structure		Materials	100% wool
	Light source: 1 x E27, max 100W (per lamp)		Dimensions	W: 170 / 200 x L: 240 / 250cm (67 / 79 x 94 / 98in)
Dimensions	H: 72 x Diam: 106cm (28 ⅜ x 42in)		Manufacturer	Nanimarquina, Spain
Manufacturer	Moooi, The Netherlands		Website	www.nanimarquina.com
Website	www.moooi.com			

Product   Textile, Repeat Dot Print (detail)
Designer   Hella Jongerius
Materials   Cotton, rayon, polyester
Dimensions   W: 140cm (55in)
Manufacturer Maharam, USA
Website   www.maharam.com
             www.jongeriuslab.com

Product   Chair, Nic
Designer   Werner Aisslinger
Materials   Polypropylene with glass fibre, chromed steel tube
Dimensions   H: 82.5 x W: 51.4 x D: 53cm (33 x 20 ⅛ x 20 ⅞in)
Manufacturer Magis SpA, Italy
Website   www.aisslinger.de

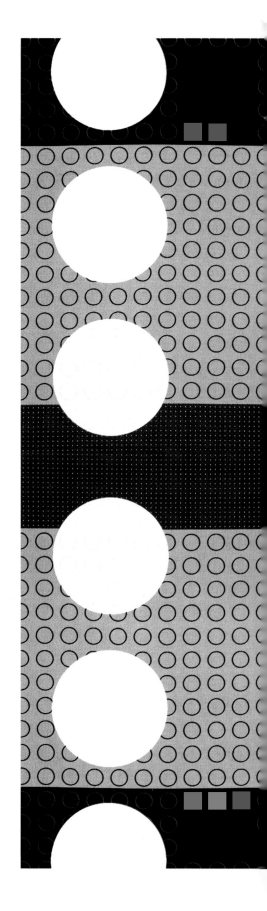

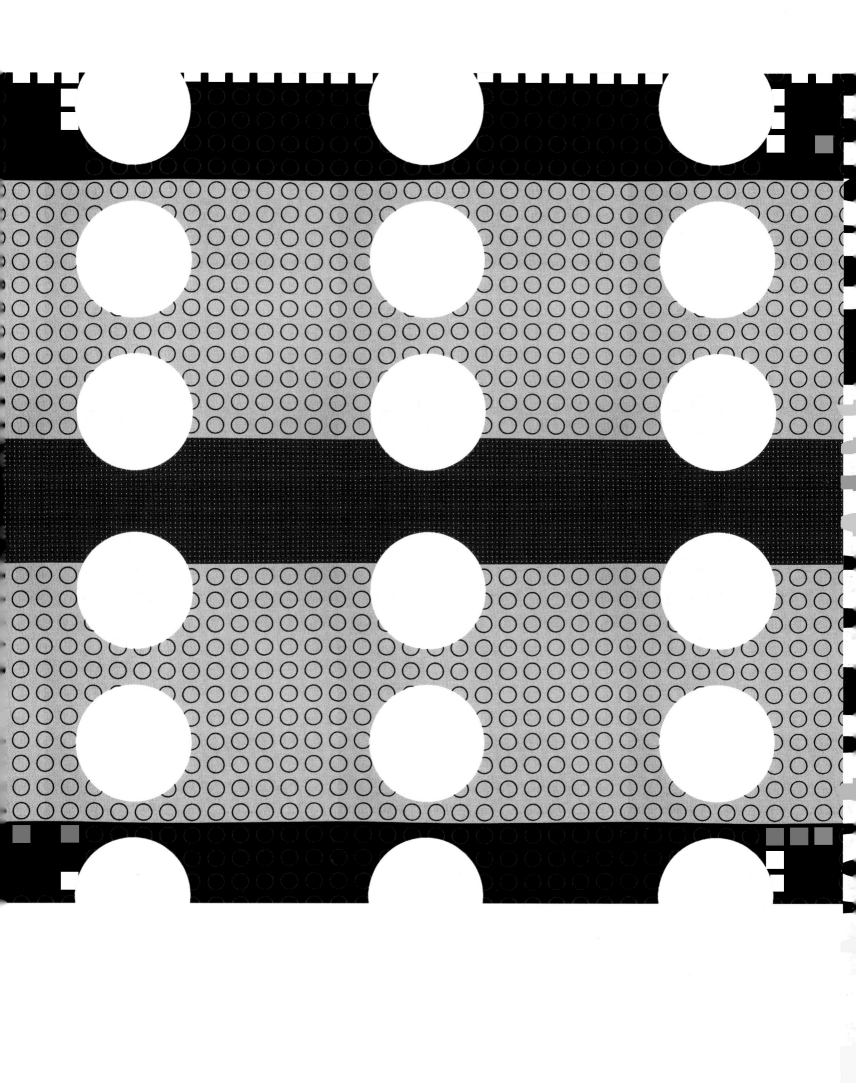

Product	Office accessories, Più
Designer	Catharina Lorenz and Steffen Kaz, Lorenz*Kaz
Materials	Bent sheet metal
Dimensions	Various sizes
Manufacturer	Zoltan Gruppo De Padova, Italy
Website	www.lorenz-kaz.com

Product   Shelves/assembly system, Platten-Bau
Designer   Florian Petri
Materials   4mm (⅛in) HPL boards
Dimensions   H: 15 / 25 / 35 / 40 x W: 40 x D: 33cm
             (5 ⅞ / 9 ⅞ / 13 ¾ / 15 ¾ x 15 ¾ x 13in)
Manufacturer Möbelbau Kaether & Weise GmbH, Germany
Website   www.kaetherundweise.de

Product	Morrison toaster
	(part of Brunch set)
Designer	Jasper Morrison
Materials	Polypropylene, stainless steel
Dimensions	H: 19.5 x L: 38.5 x W: 11cm
	(7 ⅞ x 15 ⅜ x 4 ⅜in)
Manufacturer	Rowenta, UK
Website	www.rowenta.co.uk

When asked for a word to describe how his style is perceived, Jasper Morrison had no hesitation in replying 'simple'. The brunch set for the French household appliance manufacturer Rowenta, which comprises toaster, kettle (see page 49), and coffee maker (see page 51), is just that – pure in concept, with elegant effortless lines and no gimmickry or superficial styling. At first glance the familiar white forms may even appear banal, yet closer inspection reveals a quiet intelligence, underlying subtlety and emotional creativity, qualities that have become synonymous with his work in general. Morrison believes that design should be a balance between the order demanded by a set of components and the creative inspiration that will lift an object from the workaday and appeal psychologically to the consumer. As he wrote in the introduction to *The International Design Yearbook 1999*, 'Designers must give visual and conceptual order to an object, and at the same time provide something harder to define: "objectality". Nowadays even a power drill needs to send out a message to prospective customers. While a product is born for industry, it lives the rest of its life with the person who buys it, and it's the emotional response it elicits, or "objectality", that is the key to its success.' The Rowenta range is archetypal, yet unique in its interpretation of the everyday. Classical, with a lightness of touch and effortless practicality, the pieces are essential players in the modern kitchen.

Product	Lighting, Capsule light	Product	Morrison 1.5L kettle (part of Brunch set)
Designer	Jaime Salm	Designer	Jasper Morrison
Materials	100% wool felt, steel wire, elastics and electrical components, 26W/120V fluorescent light bulb	Materials	Polypropylene, stainless steel
Dimensions	H: 30.5 x Diam: 20.3cm (12 x 8in)	Dimensions	H: 25.5 x L: 22 x W: 18.5cm (10 ¼ x 8 ⅝ x 7 ¼in)
Manufacturer	Limited batch production, Mio Company LLC, USA	Manufacturer	Rowenta, UK
Website	www.mioculture.com	Website	www.rowenta.co.uk

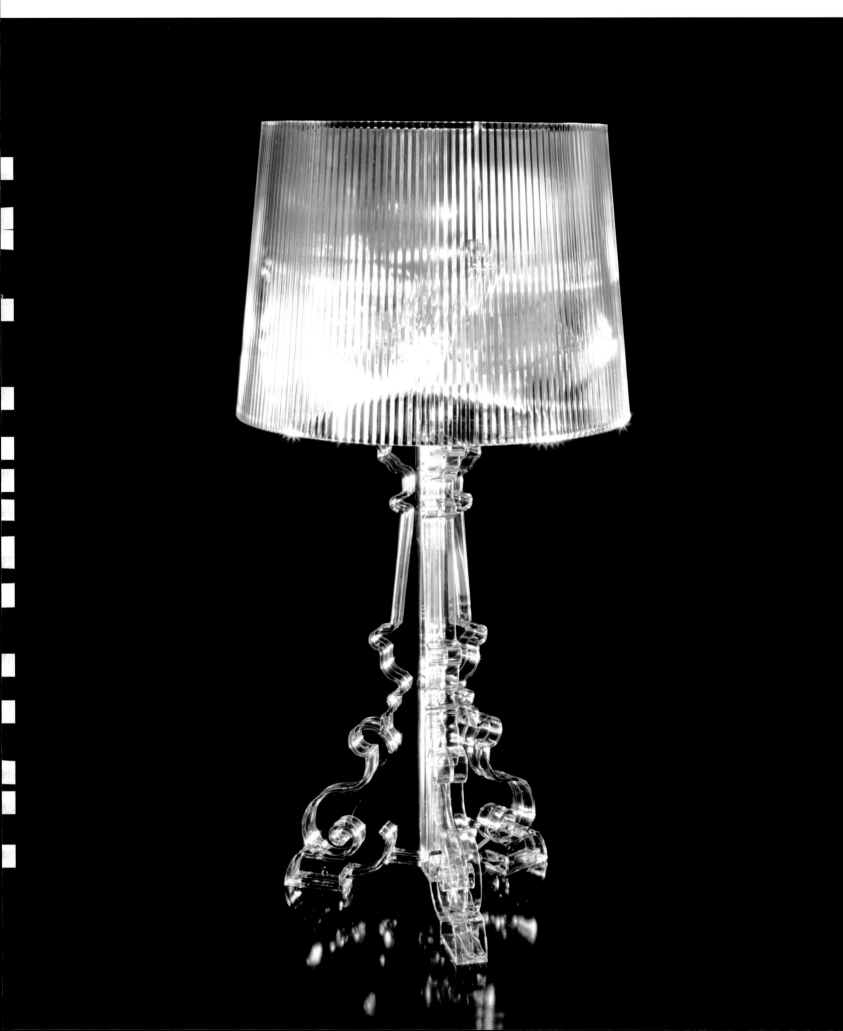

Product   Lamp, Bourgie
Designer   Ferruccio Laviani
Materials   Transparent polycarbonate
Dimensions   Diam (shade): 37 x H: 73cm (14 ⅝ x 28 ¾in)
Manufacturer Kartell SpA, Italy
Website   www.kartell.it

Product   Morrison stainless-teel thermo-jug coffee maker
             (part of Brunch set)
Designer   Jasper Morrison
Materials   Polypropylene, stainless steel
Dimensions   H: 15 x L: 29.5 x W: 33cm (5 ⅞ x 11 ¾ x 13in)
Manufacturer Rowenta, UK
Website   www.rowenta.co.uk

Morrison goes beyond the plastic hull design done before by Philippe Starck, Alessi et al. The coffee maker, in particular, casts a fresh and useful light on old routines. I love the way all elements have been snugly fitted and combined.
Chris Kabel

When I first came across this coffee machine, I just kept wondering 'Did I miss something? Or why has no one ever thought of this place to store the filters before?' It's so simple that you can't imagine that a coffee machine has ever been different.
Ineke Hans

Product   Surface pattern, 40 Extravaganza
Designer   Debbie Jane Buchan
Materials   Not applicable
Dimensions   H: 402 x W: 475cm (158 x 187in)
Manufacturer Prototype, Debbie Jane Buchan, UK

Debbie Jane Buchan's series of surface patterns was created on the advanced MAC/CAD software package, AVA CAD/CAM, a technology that allowed her to experiment with a wide range of colourways, repeats and patterns. The results of her investigation and manipulation of traditional geometric and floral imagery are designed for various applications, from car upholstery and flooring prototypes to fashion and textiles.

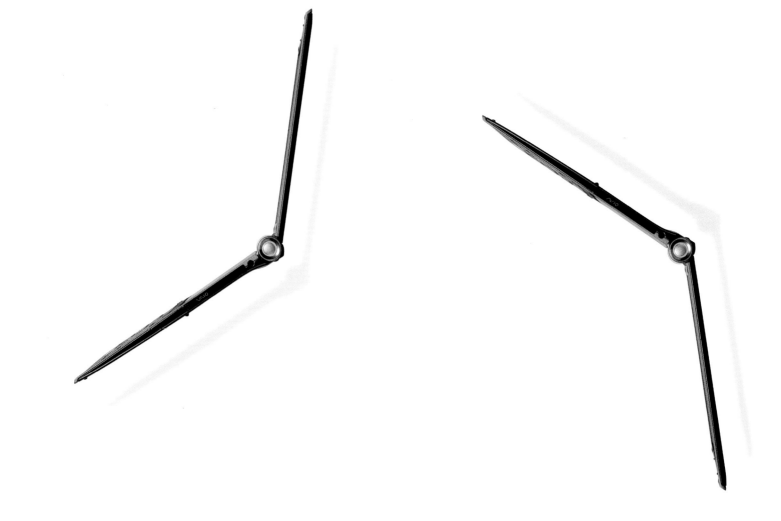

Product   VAIO notebook computer, PCG-X505
Designer   Yujin Morisawa
Materials   Carbon fibre, magnesium
Dimensions   H: 9.7 x W: 25.9 x D: 20.8cm (3 ¾ x 10 ¼ x 8 ¼in)
Manufacturer Sony Corporation, Japan
Website   www.sony.co.jp

Product	Lamp, 1totree	Product	Coctail shaker, Cosmo
Designer	Chris Kabel	Designer	Marc Newson
Materials	Cast PU resin	Materials	Crystal, PC
	Light source: 15W light bulbs	Dimensions	H: 18 x D: 8cm (7 ⅛ x 3 ⅛in)
Dimensions	Various sizes (extendable from one element	Manufacturer	Alessi, Italy
	to a complete chandelier)	Website	www.marc-newson.com
Manufacturer	Limited batch production, Chris Kabel,		
	The Netherlands		
Website	www.chriskabel.com		

Product	Lamp, Time & Space
Designer	Karim Rashid
Materials	Metal, thermoplastic resin
	Light source: compact fluorescent TC-DEL-G24, Q-2 18W
	(Class II)
Dimensions	H: 39 x W: 22 x D: 14cm x Diam. (base): 16cm
	(15 ⅜ x 8 ⅝ x 5 ½ x 6 ¼in)
Manufacturer	Artemide, Italy
Website	www.karimrashid.com

For Karim Rashid, time, space and light are inseparable. The 'Time & Space'
lamp is programmable to be alight at any time or to glow when the alarm is
activated and dim at night.

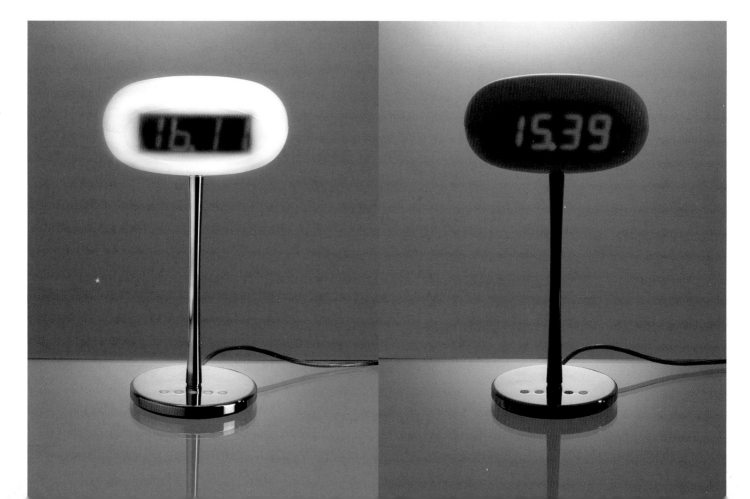

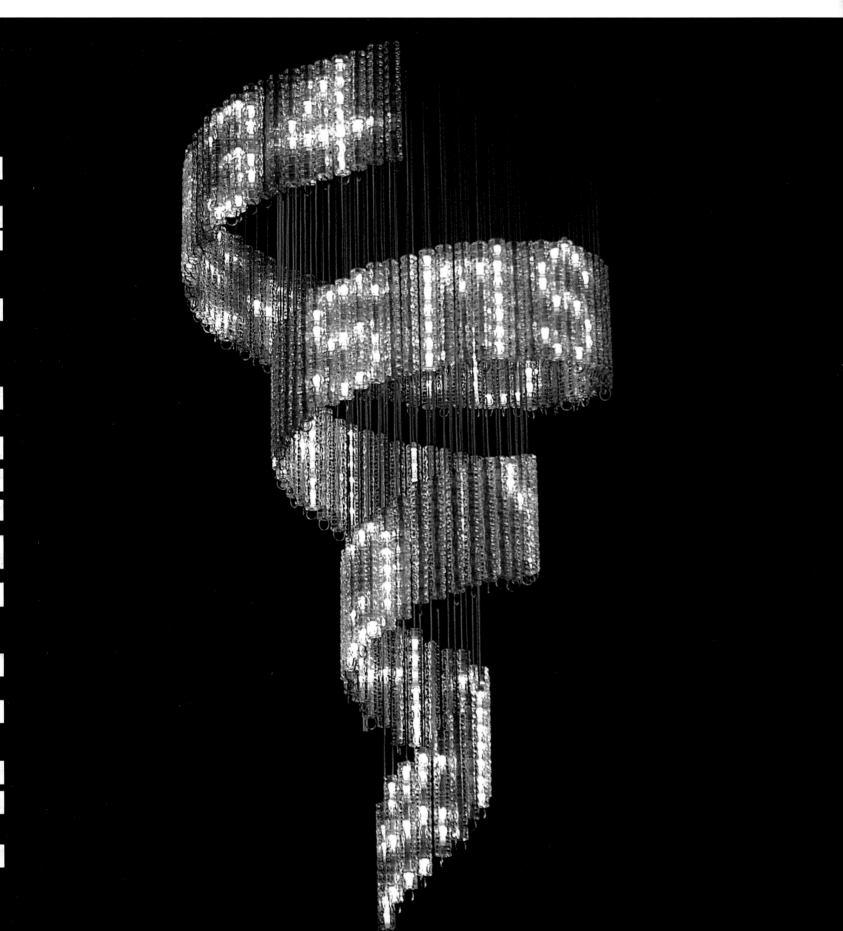

Product	Chandelier, Lolita
	(Swarovski Crystal Palace Collection 2004)
Designer	Ron Arad
Materials	Swarovski Strass crystals, white LED
Dimensions	H: 150 x Diam: 90cm (59 x 35in)
Manufacturer	Swarovski, Austria
Website	www.swarovski.com

Product	Samovar, Opera
Designer	Guido Metz & Michael Kindler
	Metz und Kindler Design
Materials	Steel, silicon
Dimensions	H: 25.5 x W: 20.5 x D: 24cm (10 x 8 ¼ x 9 ½in)
Manufacturer	WMF Aktiengesellschaft, Germany
Website	www.metz-kindler.de

Swarovski again awes us with its annual chandelier collection. Designers selected for 2004 were Ron Arad, Barber Osgerby, Yves Béhar, Tord Boontje, Constantin and Laurene Boym, David Collins and Chris Levine, Matali Crasset, Ben Jakober and Yannick Vu, Jeff Leatham and Ingo Maurer. Ron Arad's 'Lolita' took on a traditional shape, yet this interactive version receives and displays text messages. Ingo Maurer, whose name is synonymous with lighting spectaculars, didn't disappoint with 'Gio Ponti in the Sky with Diamonds' (see page 105). Shrouding his design in mystery to the very end, Maurer decided not to present an interpretation of a crystal chandelier but instead took a design classic and covered three of them in crystals and light-emitting diodes, producing a design of such fragility that it seems to float extraterrestrially.

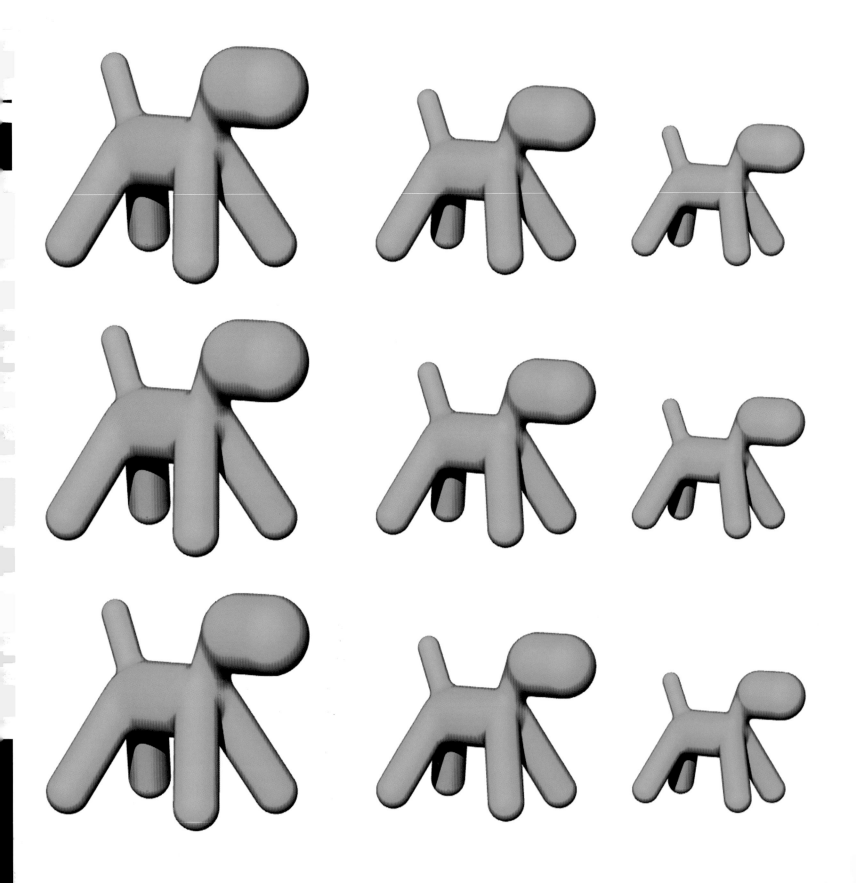

Product   Abstract plastic dog, Puppy
Designer   Eero Aarnio
Materials   Rotational moulded polyethylene
Dimensions   Various sizes
Manufacturer   Magis SpA, Italy
Website   www.magisdesign.com

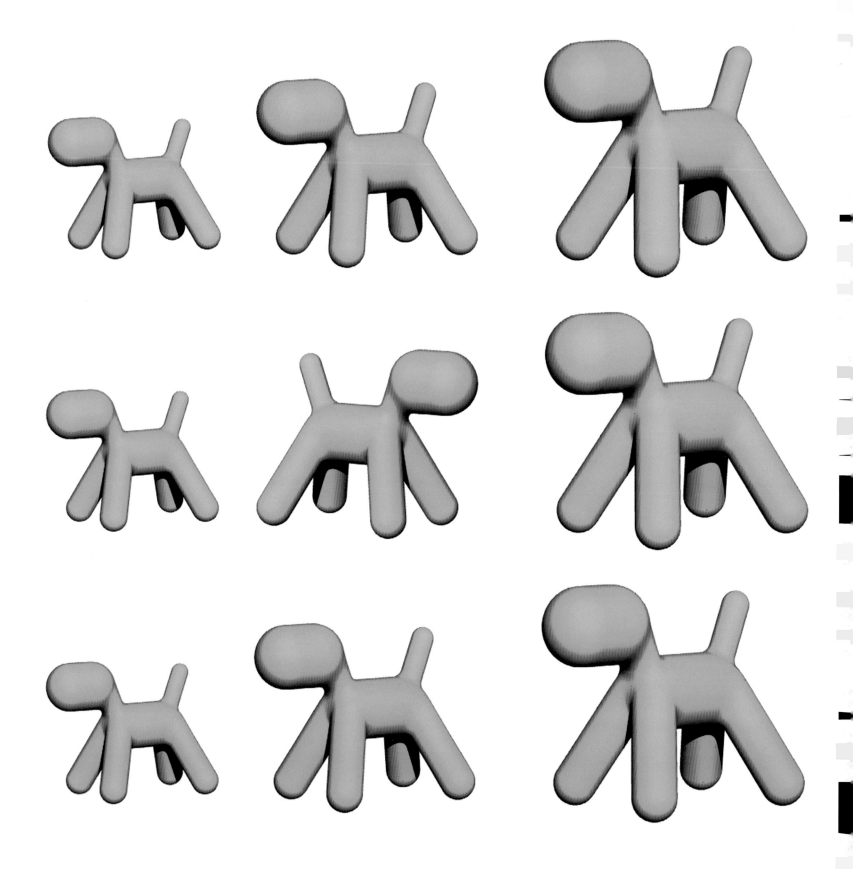

Product   Tile
Designer   Edward Barber and Jay Osgerby, Barber Osgerby
Materials   Ceramic
Dimensions   Diam: 19.5cm (7 ⅞in)
Manufacturer Limited batch production, Teamwork srl, Italy
Website   www.barberosgerby.com

Product   Chair, Ronda
Designer   Lievore, Altherr, Molina
Materials   Chrome tubular swivel central base,
              upholstered frame
Dimensions   H: (back) 74.5 x W: 63 x D: 63cm (29 ½ x 24 ¾ x 24 ¾in)
Manufacturer Andreu World, Spain
Website   www.andreuworld.com

Product	Installation at Eisava (Barcelona) and display
	dummies for Griffin Shop Soho,
	Tagging-Re-generating space
Designer	Rosario Hurtado and Roberto Feo, El Ultimo Grito
Dimensions	Not applicable
Materials	Stickers and waste materials
Manufacturer	One-off, El Ultimo Grito, UK
Website	www.elultimogrito.co.uk

Product	Fabric (curtain), Dragon
Designer	Ulf Moritz
Materials	100% polyester, plastic embossed flowers
Dimensions	W: 160cm (63in)
Manufacturer	Sahco, Germany
Website	www.ulfmoritz.com

El Ultimo Grito, the London-based design duo, was one of the contenders for the Jerwood Applied Arts Prize 2004, which was dedicated to furniture design. Their work is less about finished products and more a dialectic on how we should be encouraged to reconsider our designed environment and the objects that inhabit it. Interviewed for *The Observer Magazine*, Rosario Hurtado said 'We are about a way of thinking. Not even a philosophy, because it changes all the time. We do what we like and what we think is the right thing to do. For some people their work is about a particular shape or aesthetic, but our shapes we discover in the project. How can you know what it will look like? The idea shapes it completely. You will like it if you like our way of thinking.'

One of the concepts they exhibited at the Jerwood show is a variation on the 'Tagging' installation illustrated here. By covering a space – both the architecture and the purpose-built furniture within it – with specially designed stickers, Feo and Hurtado aim to give a coherent identity to a disparate set of objects within their setting, regenerating an interior landscape from waste materials and objects. The installation at the Eisava School in Barcelona was developed in collaboration with the students, who made furniture from reclaimed objects found in skips. The stickers are inspired by Gaudí mosaics.

Product   Flower vase, Luna
Designer   Masanobu Ido
Materials   Porcelain
Dimensions   H: 16 x W: 16 x D: 16cm (6 ¼ x 6 ¼ x 6 ¼in)
Manufacturer Limited batch production, M-Pro, Japan

Product   Surface pattern, 72 daisy red
Designer   Debbie Jane Buchan
Materials   Not applicable
Dimensions   H: 25 x W: 23cm (9 ⅞ x 9in)
Manufacturer Prototype, Debbie Jane Buchan, UK

Product   Office desk system, Double You
Designer   Hannes Wettstein
Materials   Galvanized steel plate, lacquered in three different colours
               or covered with veneer, Cordura textile or PU skin
Dimensions   Various sizes
Manufacturer   Bulo, Belgium
Website   www.bulo.com

Product	Modular series of vases, Be Your Own Florist
Designer	Kiki van Eijk
Materials	Stainless steel
Dimensions	H: 35 x L: 21 x W: 14cm (13 ¾ x 8 ¼ x 5 ½ in)
Manufacturer	Prototype, Kiki van Eijk, The Netherlands
Website	www.kikiworld.nl

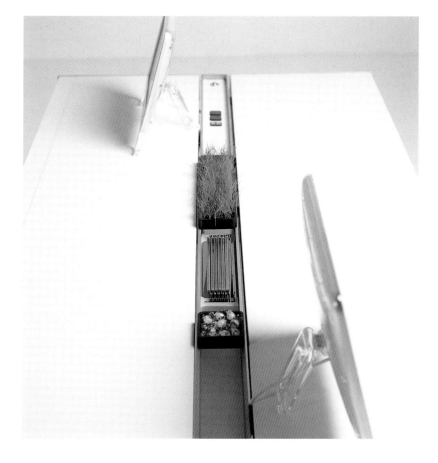

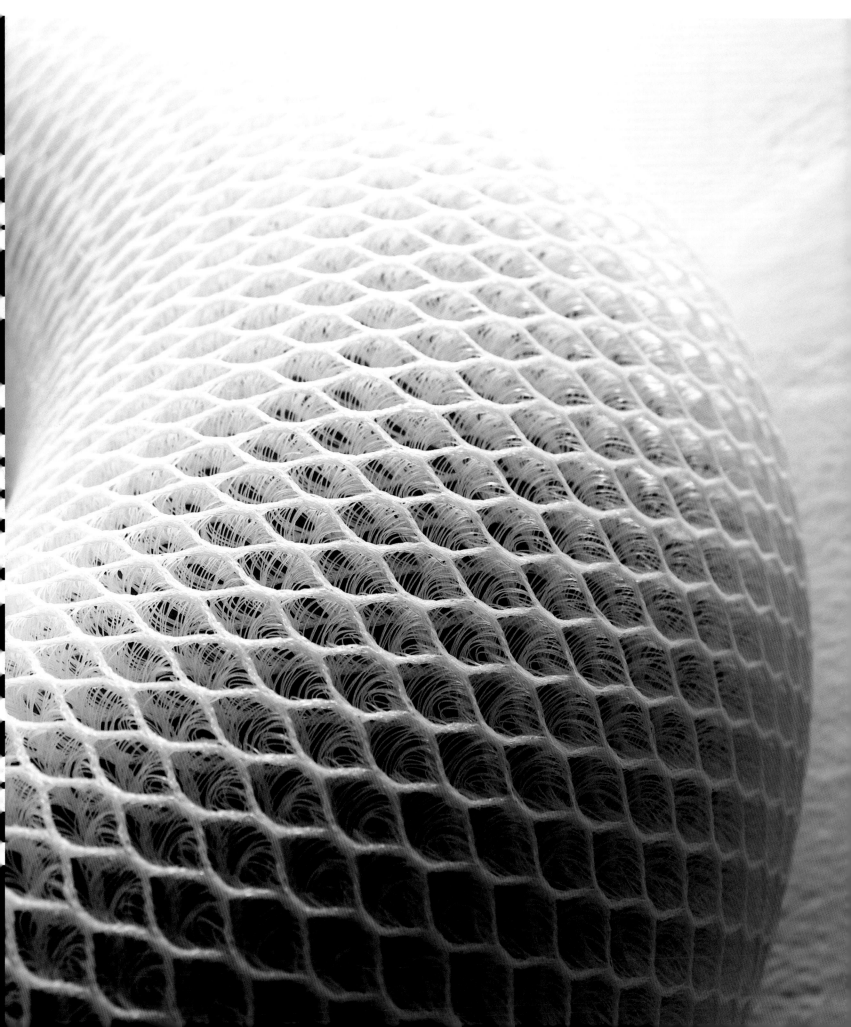

Product	Net cushion, Ami-Zabuton
Designer	Sachio Hihara
Materials	Three-dimensional nylon fibre, rubber
Dimensions	Diam: 80 x H: 25cm (31 x 9 ⅞in)
Manufacturer	Prototype, Sachio Hihara, Japan
Website	www.sachio.jp

'Ami-Zabuton' (net cushion in Japanese) was conceived as a piece of furniture that falls halfway between the traditional Japanese floor cushion and the western chair. It consists of a new material, 'Fusion', produced by Asahi Kasei Fibers. The three-dimensional textile is wrapped around a rubber ring and changes form as it is stretched.

Product	Sunglasses, Physics
Designer	Ross Lovegrove
Materials	Titanium, magnesium and aluminium alloy with silicone nose bridge and polycarbonate lenses
Dimensions	12 x 2 x 4.5cm (4 ¾ x ¾ x 1 ¾in)
Manufacturer	Tag Heuer, Switzerland
Website	www.tagheuer.com

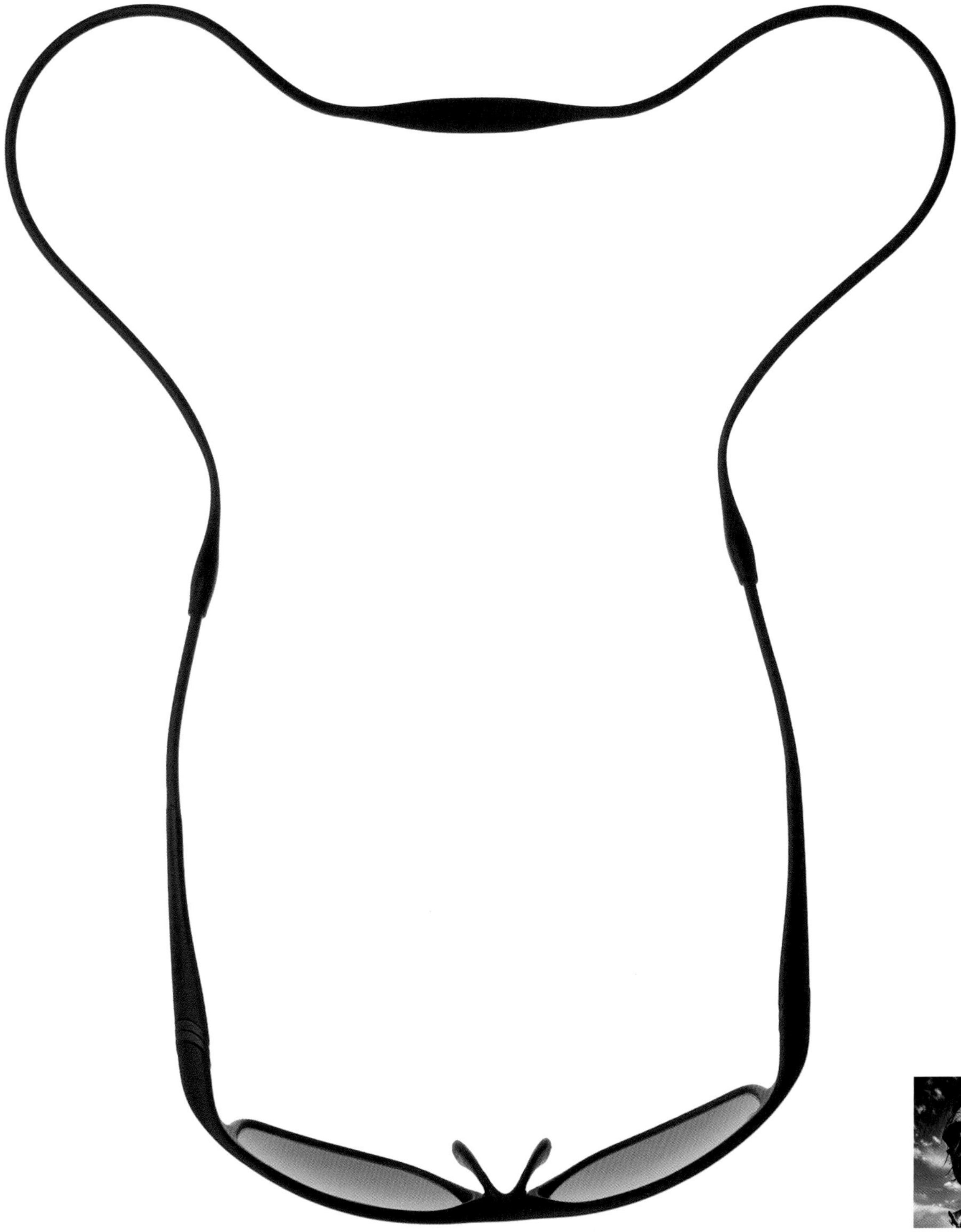

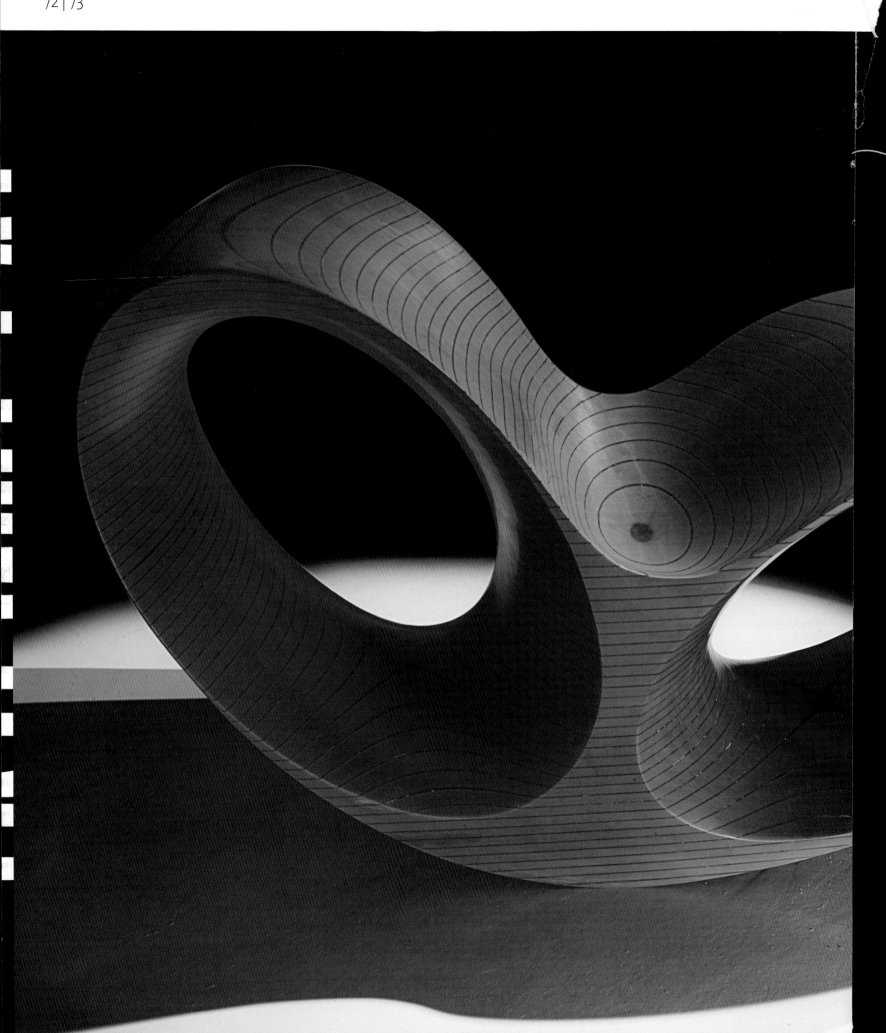

Product	Rocking daybed, Oh Void 2
Designer	Ron Arad
Materials	Corian, coloured glue
Dimensions	H: 123 x W: 47 x L: 193cm (48 x 18 ½ x 76in)
Manufacturer	Limited batch production, The Gallery Mourmans, The Netherlands
Website	www.ronarad.com

Ron Arad's reworking of his 'Oh Void' chair in Corian illustrates a quite different quality of the material from his 'Lo-rez-dolores' table (see page 23). Many designers use same-coloured adhesive to create invisible seams. Arad has turned this process on its head and used contrasting colours in the adhesive to produce a pinstripe effect, each join becoming part of the surface patterning.

Product	Armchair, Bloomy
Designer	Patricia Urquiola
Materials	Steel, flame-retardant cold-expanded foam
Dimensions	H: 75 (seat: 46) x W: 58 x D: 58cm
	(29 ½ / 18 ⅛ x 22 ⅞ x 22 ⅞in)
Manufacturer	Moroso, Italy
Website	www.moroso.it

Patricia Urquiola is the designer of the year. Her ubiquity at the Milan Furniture Fair was staggering. I can't imagine there are many major furniture manufacturers with whom she is not currently collaborating – Driade, B&B Italia, Kartell, Agape and Moroso are just a few of the names with which she is linked. She has sat on illustrious design panels, was the Guest of Honour at the Stockholm Furniture Fair and has been awarded prizes herself for her elegant yet unfussy, simple yet eye-catching pieces (most recently the 2003 Best System Award for her Fjord Collection for Moroso). And in 2005, along with Hella Jongerius, Urquiola will offer us her concept for the perfect domestic interior in the Ideal House Installation – the most talked about event of the Cologne Furniture Fair. Unlike many names that the fickle media promote one season and cast into obscurity the next, Urquiola's pedigree will ensure her a place among those set to stay. Her public image has been built up gradually; it is not dependent on press hype and as such will not be tied down to a period or nailed to a style.

Urquiola graduated from the Madrid Polytechnic, then moved to Italy and completed her education under Achille Castiglioni at the Milan Polytechnic. Until she set up her own Milan-based studio in 2001, she worked for Vico Magistretti, de Padova and Lissoni Associati, names associated less with the vagaries of fashion than with commercial and classical Italian design. From these experiences she has built up a strong head for business and a thorough knowledge of the manufacturing industry, while maintaining a personal style that is a blend of Spanish minimalism and Italian flamboyance. Among those she admires she lists more avant-garde designers – Konstantin Grcic, Jasper Morrison, Marcel Wanders and the Bouroullec brothers – all of whom show sound commercial acumen while producing, like Urquiola, simple pieces with tiny details that have an emotional kick and provoke discussion.

Her work is functional and unembellished – 'My designs don't need an explanation; they have to speak for themselves' – drawing inspiration from works of art, from travel, fashion and everyday life. She strongly believes that every piece of furniture should have a context and not be produced in isolation. Although she admires the more conceptual designers so popular at the moment, she considers that a successful design should always bear the customer in mind. Her furniture is user-friendly, sensuous and accommodating, designed to mould to the body and fit in with the architecture that surrounds it. 'I do want my work to be personal, but I'm not out to make an attention-getting design statement'. 'Bloomy', which follows the current trend for organic-shaped furniture, was inspired by a desert flower that Urquiola spotted while on holiday.

Patricia & I had a fight. to me this was the most beautifull chair of the year. I hope I get one from moroso

marcel

Product	Vase/candlestick, Night and Day
	(part of the Cornerwork series)
Designer	Michael Rowe
Materials	925 silver
Dimensions	H: 34 x W: 33 x D: 20cm (13 ⅜ x 13 x 7 ⅞in)
Manufacturer	Limited batch production, Michael Rowe

This ingenious vase and candleholder design, from the 'Cornerwork' series, is one of a selection of products that exploits the geometry of angles in interior spaces.

Product	Silk hanging, Water Rose
Designer	Tord Boontje
Materials	Digitally printed silk
Dimensions	150 x 500 cm (59 x 197in)
Manufacturer	Prototype, Tord Boontje/Moroso/Isa
Website	www.tordboontje.com

Product   Cutlery set, Asta
Designer   Alessandro Mendini
Materials   18/10 stainless steel
Dimensions   Various sizes
Manufacturer   Alessi SpA, Italy
Website   www.alessi.com

Product   Chair, UNO
Designer   Bartoli Design and Fauciglietti Engineering
Materials   R 606 'leather'
Dimensions   H: 79 (seat: 44) x W: 48 x D: 45cm
             (31 / 17 ⅜ x 18 ⅞ x 17 ¾in)
Manufacturer Segis SpA, Italy
Website   www.segis.it

Like the outline of a chair drawn by a child and produced in primary colours, the form of 'UNO' is intentionally elementary in order that we focus our attention on the innovative material in which it is manufactured. R606 takes its inspiration from nature. Like the epidermis, its outer skin protects the body within. Co-moulded in a single production process, the chemically composed, tight-celled skin is combined with the soft urethane-foam padding inside, resulting in a sturdy and water-resistant structure, hard on the surface yet soft to the touch and with a flexibility never before achieved by manufacturing process.

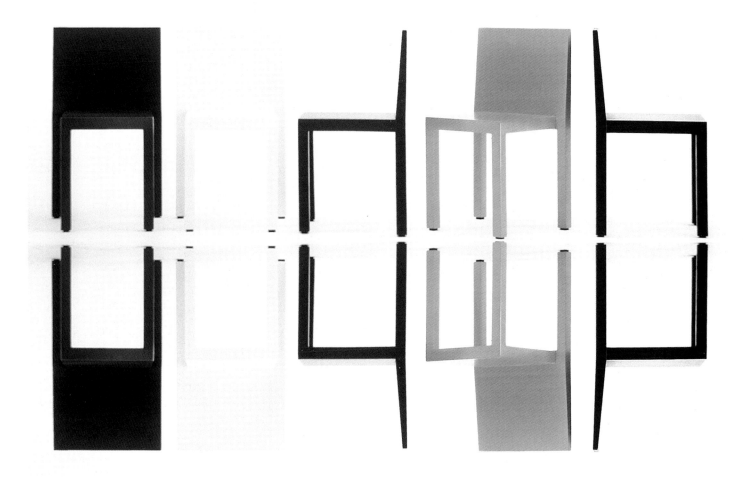

Product   Radiator system and towel drier, Velum
Designer   Perry King and Santiago Miranda with C. Knox
Materials   Steel and extruded aluminium
Dimensions   Various sizes
Manufacturer   Runtal (Zehnder Group), Switzerland
Website   www.kingmiranda.com

Creating a feature out of a necessity, King and Miranda have developed an innovative heating system that employs curtains of aluminium to radiate heat. Joris Laarman for Droog Design has gone a step further and produced a concrete sculptural radiator of baroque splendour (see pages 114–15).

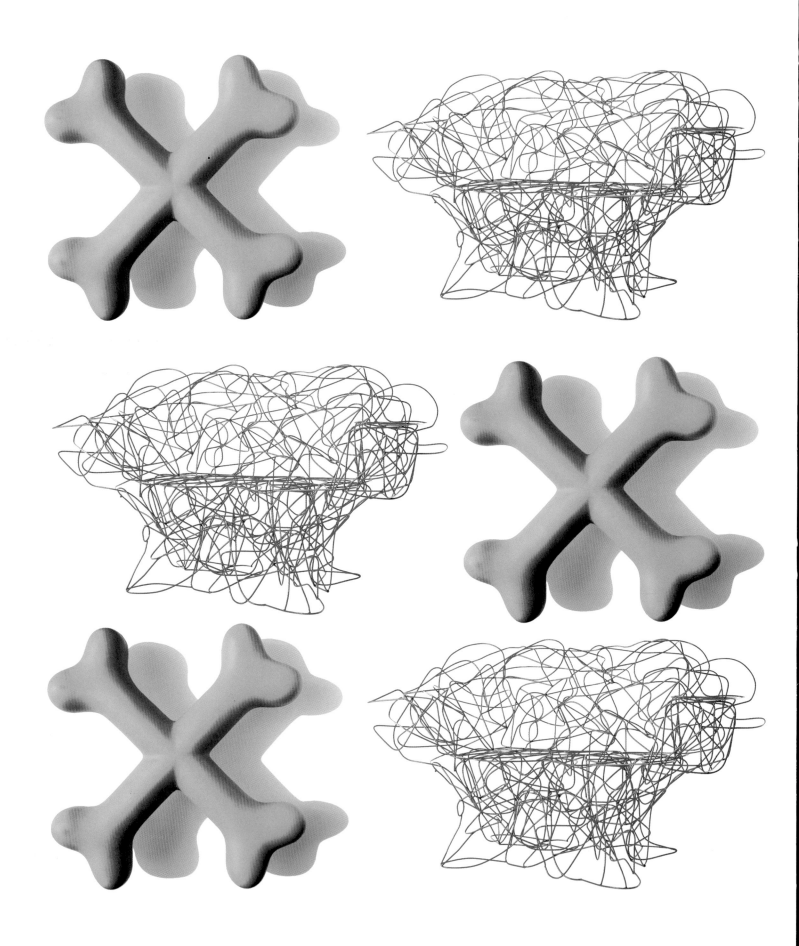

Product	Dog toy, DXG BXNE
Designer	Karim Rashid
Materials	Non-toxic polymer
Dimensions	W: 16.5 x D: 2.5cm (6 ½ x 1in)
Manufacturer	For the dogs, Canada
Website	www.karimrashid.com

Product	Armchair, Corallo
Designer	Ferdinando and Humberto Campana
Materials	Iron
Dimensions	H: 140 x W: 100 x D: 90cm (55 x 39 x 35in)
Manufacturer	Edra SpA, Italy
Website	www.edra.com

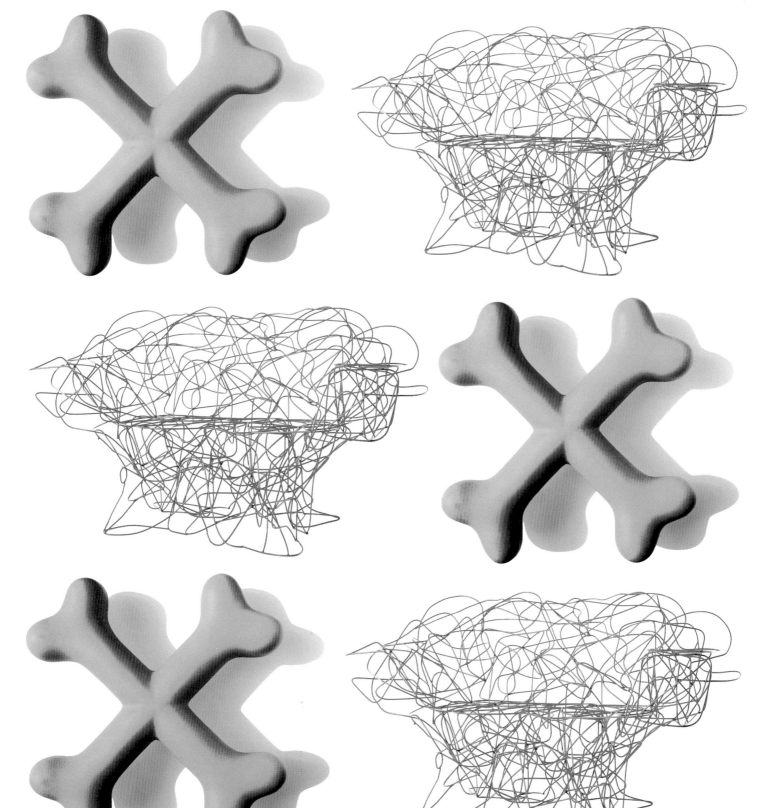

Product	Dog toy, DXG BXNE
Designer	Karim Rashid
Materials	Non-toxic polymer
Dimensions	W: 16.5 x D: 2.5cm (6 ½ x 1in)
Manufacturer	For the dogs, Canada
Website	www.karimrashid.com

Product	Armchair, Corallo
Designer	Ferdinando and Humberto Campana
Materials	Iron
Dimensions	H: 140 x W: 100 x D: 90cm (55 x 39 x 35in)
Manufacturer	Edra SpA, Italy
Website	www.edra.com

Product   Digital camera, Digital Ixus i
Designer   Masataka Isomoto
Materials   Aluminium alloy, stainless steel, PC/ABS
Dimensions   H: 4.7 x W: 9.03 x D: 1.85cm (1¾ x 3½ x ¾in)
Manufacturer   Design Center, Canon Inc, Japan
Website   www.canon.co.jp

Product   Vases, Gem Group
Designer   Kate Hume
Materials   Glass
Dimensions   Various sizes
Manufacturer One-off, Kate Hume Glass, The Netherlands

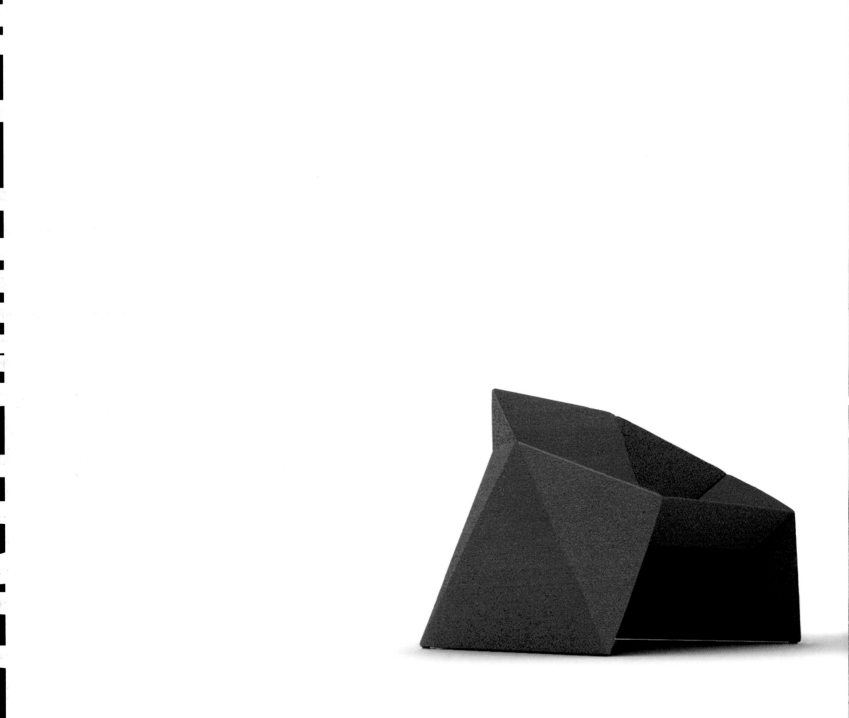

Product	Sofa and armchair, 2
Designer	Dodo Arslan
Materials	Steel-pipe frame, polyurethane upholstery, fabric
Dimensions	H: 78 x L: (sofa) 188 / (armchair) 100 x D: 88cm
	(31 x 74 / 39 x 35in)
Manufacturer	Prototype, Dodo Arslan
Website	www.arslan.it

Product   Fabric (curtain/panel), Nightingale
Designer   Ulf Moritz
Materials   57% silk, 43% acetate
Dimensions   W: 145cm (57in)
Manufacturer Sahco, Germany
Website   www.ulfmoritz.com

Product   Textile, Repeat Dot Print (detail)
Designer   Hella Jongerius
Materials   Cotton, rayon, polyester
Dimensions   W: 140cm (55in)
Manufacturer Maharam, USA
Website   www.jongeriuslab.com
             www.maharam.com

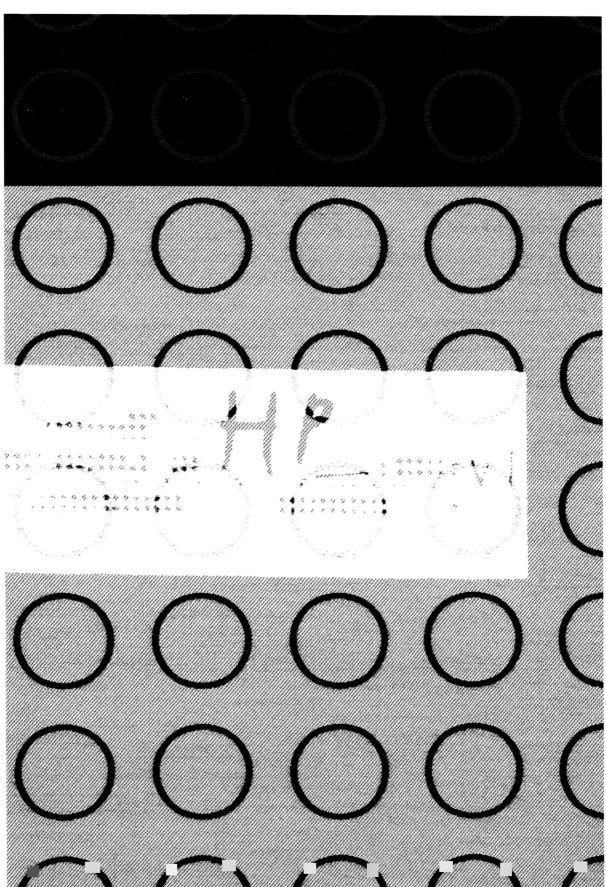

Product   Modular sideboard, Box-Rounded
Designer   Hannes Rohringer
Materials   Wood, lacquer
Dimensions   H: 107.3 x W: 50 x L: 155cm (42 x 19 ⅝ x 61in)
Manufacturer   Streitner GmbH, Austria
Website   www.streitner.at

Product   Drawer unit on wheels, Groove
Designer   Christian Ghion
Materials   Rotation-moulded plastic
Dimensions   W: 180 x H: 50 x D: 56.9cm (71 x 19 ⅝ x 22 ½in)
Manufacturer   Driade, Italy
Website   www.christianghion.com
               www.driade.com

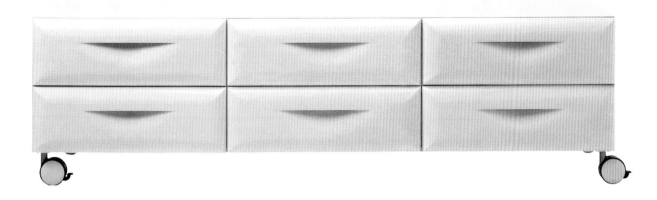

Product   Combination plates, Divide
Designer   Masatoshi Sakaegi
Materials   Porcelain
Dimensions   H: 2.6 x L: 20 x D: 8.5cm (1 x 7 ⅞ x 3 ⅜in)
Manufacturer Sakaegi Design Studio, Japan

Product	DNA spiral staircase
Designer	Ross Lovegrove
Materials	Steps in bladder-moulded GRP and mono-directional carbon fibre. Handrail in solid bladder-moulded carbon fibre
Dimensions	H: 400 x Diam: 240cm (158 x 94in)
Manufacturer	Ross Lovegrove, UK

Ross Lovegrove's leitmotif staircase spirals like a double-helix from the top floor to the hollowed-out basement of his recent studio refurbishment in London's Notting Hill. Lovegrove is best known for his biomorphic designs and intelligent use of innovative materials, processes and technologies, and the staircase echoes the sensibilities of earlier designs such as the bleached-bones 'Go' chair for Bernhardt and, even more so, his 2004 exhibition 'Designosaurus'. Taking what he refers to as 'organic minimalism' to the extreme, Lovegrove re-engineered the dinosaur skeleton as architecture, producing life-size models in lightweight polystyrene. Skeletally, the twisted spine of his studio staircase is obviously borrowed from the flowing forms of nature. Lovegrove makes collections of objects that he uses as source material and inspiration, including fossils, bones, castings and sculptures – 'fat-free forms', as he calls them.

Although the staircase is site specific, Lovegrove is researching ways of remodelling it to manufacture a product that could have other commercial applications. To create the fragile pedal-shaped treads and the delicate outline of the original, however, involved a highly specialized process and the development of a unique material. The staircase is fabricated from an eight-millimetre (⅓in) deep matt fibreglass, reinforced by unidirectional carbon, while the high-quality finish was obtained by the bladder-moulding technique used on Formula One cars. This process involves a composite of gas and injection moulding, and Lovegrove also invested money in the creation of a specialized tool made from seven-part aluminium, into which an inflatable rubber membrane has been introduced. This forces the resin against the mould walls creating an extra smooth and even result. As with many of his designs, the form was developed on a stereolithographic modelling machine, which enabled Lovegrove to visualize in three dimensions and to explore the holistic qualities of the object. This was followed up by a series of trial-and-error tests before the elegant profile, which has a delicacy that belies its strength, was reached. Each step, attached to the central steel post by a single nut, can carry 420 kilograms (924lb). The handrail runs independently of the main staircase and is made from carbon fibre. Initially Lovegrove had shied away from a spiral, thinking the form 'banal'. In the end, after research into linear and other possibilities, he adopted this typology to make the most of the limited space available yet produce a feature staircase. Interviewed by Deyan Sudjic for *Domus*, Lovegrove pointed out, 'It has a practical value. The spiral could have been smaller and tighter and still worked. But because it saves space, you can afford to be much more generous'.

Product   Bowls, Love/Big Love/Super Love
Designer   Miriam Mirri
Materials   PMMA, stainless steel 18/10
Dimensions   Various sizes
Manufacturer Alessi SpA, Italy
Website   www.alessi.com

Product   Mikro-House (from the Mikro series)
Designer   Sam Buxton
Materials   0.15mm-thick hard-rolled stainless steel
Dimensions   Folded: 8 x 8 x 8 cm (3 ⅛ x 3 ⅛ x 3 ⅛in)
Manufacturer Worldwide Co., UK
Website   www.sambuxton.com

The Mikro series developed from a business card that Sam Buxton designed. Wanting to show his work directly from his pocket, this card transformed from flat into a 3D object that could be kept. The process he uses is industrial acid etching. Commonly used in the electronics industry, it allows Sam to manufacture at high volume while also achieving fine detailing. The stainless steel sheet stays rigid when folded.

Along the same lines, the 'HUB' project commissioned by the Craft Centre in Sleaford used the technique to create a commissioning centre. Stainless steel was laser cut, forming furniture, magazine racks and even coat hangers from the walls of a cube-shaped room.

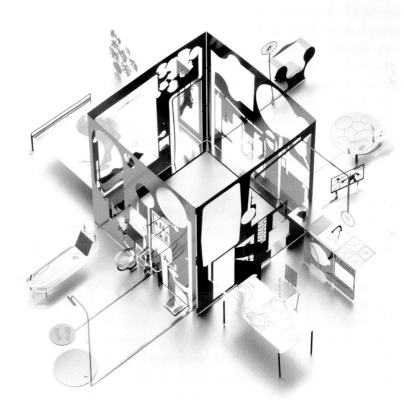

Product   Long-lasting lipstick, Lipfinity
Manufacturer Max Factor, USA
Website   www.maxfactor.com

24-hour kiss – and it works! Thanks!
Wieki Somers

kissing is one of our best habits!
this lipstick is great
sticks better, makes no stains!
I love the real important
developments in design.
marcel

Product   Corner bench, Together
Designer   EOOS
Materials   Steel, foam, leather
Dimensions   H: 80 x W: 68 x L: 245–313cm
              (31 x 26 ¾ x 96–123in)
Manufacturer Walter Knoll, Germany
Website   www.eoos.com

Product   Furniture, Equipment
Designer   Sam Hecht and Kim Colin
Materials   Aluminium, Corian composite
Dimensions   H: 235 x W: 156 x D: 80cm (93 x 61 x 31in)
Manufacturer Prototype, Whirlpool Europe, Italy
Website   www.industrialfacility.co.uk

Product   Bar stool, Little Gubi
Designer   Boris Berlin & Poul Christiansen, Komplot Design
Materials   3D veneer, steel tube or solid rod frames, upholstery
Dimensions   H: 88 / (seat) 75 x W: 44 x D: 45cm
               (35 / 29 ½ x 17 ⅜ x 17 ¾in)
Manufacturer   Gubi, Denmark
Website   www.komplot.dk

Product   Surface pattern, 64 Mixed Posy 10
Designer   Debbie Jane Buchan
Materials   Not applicable
Dimensions   H: 14 x W: 12cm (5 ½ x 4 ¾in)
Manufacturer   Prototype, Debbie Jane Buchan, UK

Product   Wireless speaker
Designer   Kyoko Inoda + Nils Sveje Architecture and Design Studio
Materials   Resin-reinforced chalk
Dimensions   (Speaker) D: 14.3 x W: 20 x L: 20cm
               (56 x 7 ⅞ x 7 ⅞in) H: (with leg) 80cm (31in)
Manufacturer   Limited batch production, One Off, Italy
Website   www.inoda.com

The Japanese/Danish duo Kyoko Inoda and Nils Sveje have updated 'His Master's Voice'. Their wireless speaker may look like a tennis ball, but it can play the tones of any musical device from stereo to computer, wherever and whenever needed.

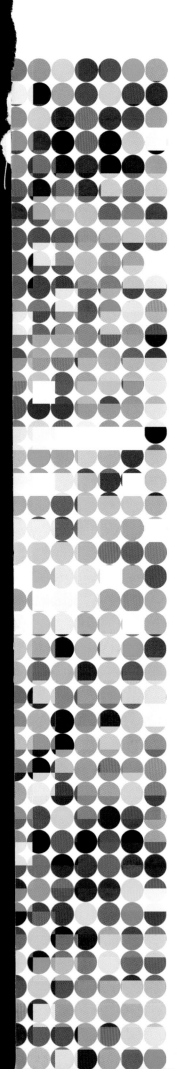

Product   Surface pattern, 85 Circle Pattern
Designer   Debbie Jane Buchan
Materials   Not applicable
Dimensions   H: 22 x W: 23cm (8 ⅝ x 9in)
Manufacturer Prototype, Debbie Jane Buchan, UK

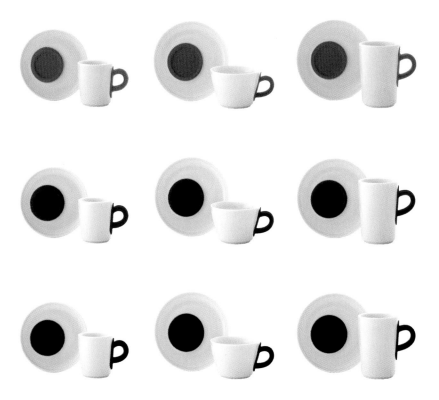

Product   Porcelain with textile coating, Touch!
Designer   Thilo Schwer, Speziell Produktgestaltung,
             and Barbara Schmidt
Materials   Polyamide, porcelain
Dimensions   Various sizes
Manufacturer Kahla/Thüringen Porzellan GmbH, Germany
Website   www.kahlaporzellan.com

Product   Ceramic bowl and cover, Pottery
Designer   Vincent Van Duysen
Materials   Ceramic, sandblasted oak
Dimensions   Various sizes
Manufacturer When Objects Work, Belgium
Website   www.whenobjectswork.com

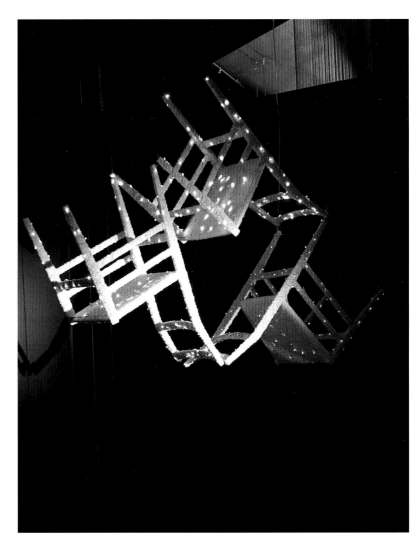

Product   Chandelier, Gio Ponti in the Sky with Diamonds
              (Swarovski Crystal Palace Collection 2004)
Designer   Ingo Maurer
Materials   Swarovski Strass crystals, white LED
Dimensions   L: 160 x W: 37 x H: 110cm (63 x 14 ⅝ x 43in)
Manufacturer Swarovski, Austria
Website   www.swarovski.com

Product   Ceramics, Ryker
Designer   Lucy. D
Materials   Porcelain, platin glaze
Dimensions   Various sizes
Manufacturer Limited batch production, Lucy. D, Austria
Website   www.lucyd.com

'Ryker' – recycled ceramic – developed from Karin Stiglmair's and Barbara
Ambrosz' desire to reuse odd pieces of crockery. By adding a unifying visual
element to china of various sizes and shapes, they have created completely
new dinner services. The rim of each plate is glazed with platinum and gives
a square shape to the normally round plate.

Product   Ceramic tile, Mosa Terra Maestricht
Designer   Royal Mosa Design Team
Materials   Unglazed ceramic tiles
Dimensions   Various sizes
Manufacturer   Royal Mosa, The Netherlands
Website   www.mosa.nl

Product   Rug, Cuks
Designer   Nani Marquina
Materials   100% wool
Dimensions   Various sizes
Manufacturer Nanimarquina, Spain
Website   www.nanimarquina.com

Product	CD player, Bookshelf CD Player
Designer	Muji Design Team
Materials	Plastics, electronics
Dimensions	H: 31.5 x W: 7.8 x D: 20.4cm (12 ⅝ x 3 ⅛ x 7 ⅞in)
Manufacturer	Muji, Japan
Website	www.muji.co.uk

Product	MP3 player, iPod mini
Designer	Apple Industrial Design Group (Design Team: Bart Andre, Danny Coster, Daniele De Iuliis, Richard Howarth, Jonathan Ive, Duncan Kerr, Shin Nishibori, Matthew Rohrbach, Doug Satzger, Carl Seid, Christopher Stringer, Eugene Whang; CAD Team: Carlos Ragudo, Carter Multz, Christopher Hood, Fred Simon, Irene Chan-Jones, Ken Provost, Mas Watanabe)
Materials	Anodized aluminium
Dimensions	H: 9.14 x W: 5.08 x L: 12.7cm (3 ½ x 2 x 4 ⅞in)
Manufacturer	Apple Computer, Inc., USA
Website	www.apple.com

Product	Espresso coffee maker (from coffee system series), More Kult
Designer	Guido Metz & Michael Kindler, Metz und Kindler Design
Materials	Steel, polypropylene
Dimensions	H: 14.2 x W: 10.4 x D: 14cm (5 ½ x 4 ⅛ x 5 ½in)
Manufacturer	WMF Aktiengesellschaft, Germany
Website	www.metz-kindler.de.

Product   Concept car, Fiat Panda Alessi
Designer   Redesign: Stefano Giovannoni
Materials   Not applicable
Dimensions   L: 353.8 x W: 157.8–158.9 x H: 154–157.8cm
                (139 x 62–63 x 61–62in)
Manufacturer   Fiat Auto, Italy
Website   www.alessi.com

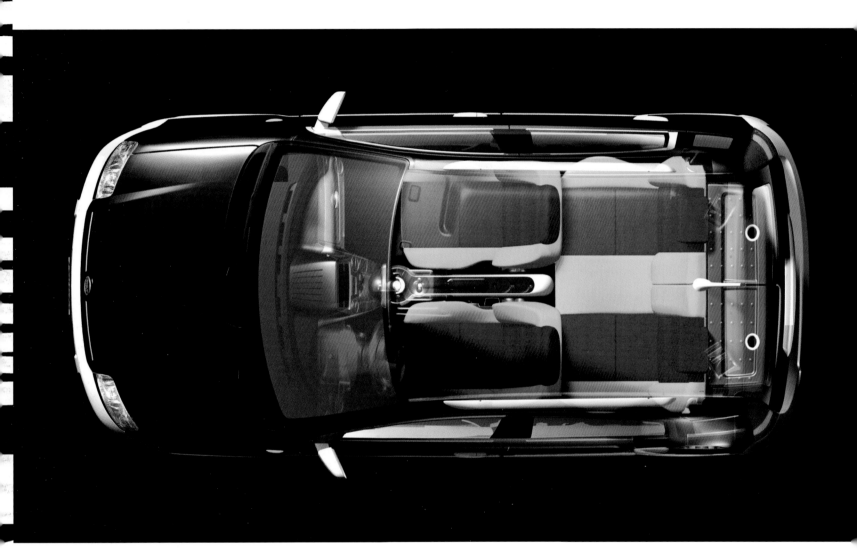

Product   Candelabra, Pearl Candelabra
Designer   Tord Boontje
Materials   Powder-coated steel, glass, faux pearls
Dimensions   55 x H: 100 cm x L: 350 cm (21 ⅝ x 39 x 138in)
Manufacturer One-off for Ian Schrager, Tord Boontje Studio, UK
Website   www.tordboontje.com

Product	Surface pattern, 65 Mixed Posy 11(coloured)	Product	Surface pattern, 67 Mixed Posy 13 (white)
Designer	Debbie Jane Buchan	Designer	Debbie Jane Buchan
Materials	Not applicable	Materials	Not applicable
Dimensions	H: 14 x W: 12cm (5 ½ x 4 ¾in)	Dimensions	H: 14 x W: 12cm (5 ½ x 4 ¾in)
Manufacturer	Prototype, Debbie Jane Buchan, UK	Manufacturer	Prototype, Debbie Jane Buchan, UK

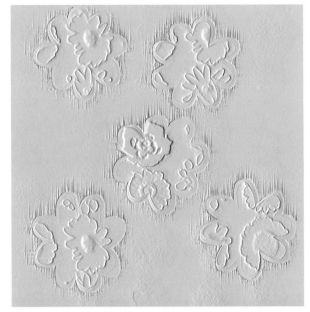

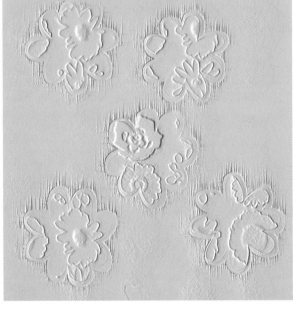

Product	Floor clothes-stand, Dodici	Product	Table, Twisted metal table
Designer	James Irvine	Designer	Véronique Maire and Patrick de Glo de Besses,
Materials	Steel		IK Design
Dimensions	W: (base) 40 x L: (base) 40 x H: 170cm (15 ¾ x 15 ¾ x 67in)	Materials	Twisted metal
Manufacturer	Pallucco, Italy	Dimensions	H: 74 x L: 205 x W: 76cm (29 ⅛ x 81 x 29 ⅞in)
Website	www.pallucco.com	Manufacturer	Prototype, Cockpit/VIA, France

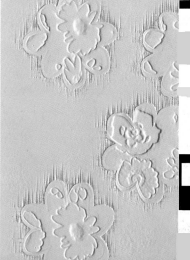

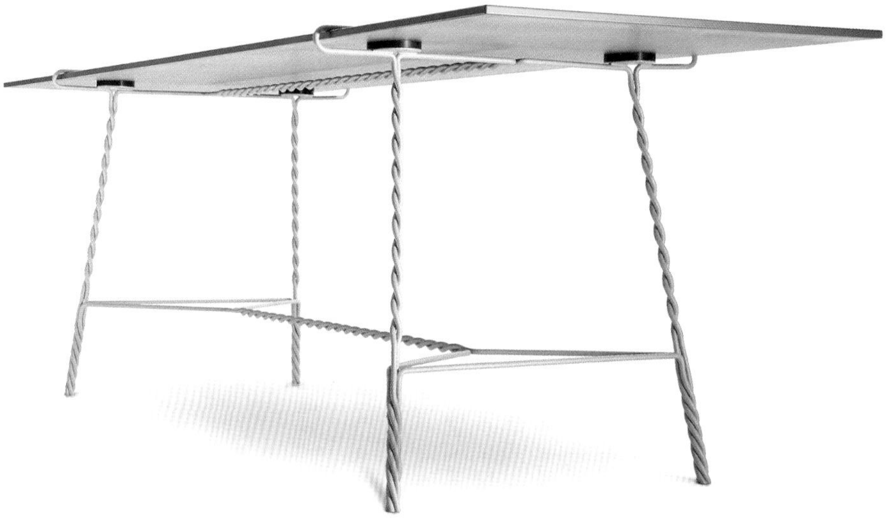

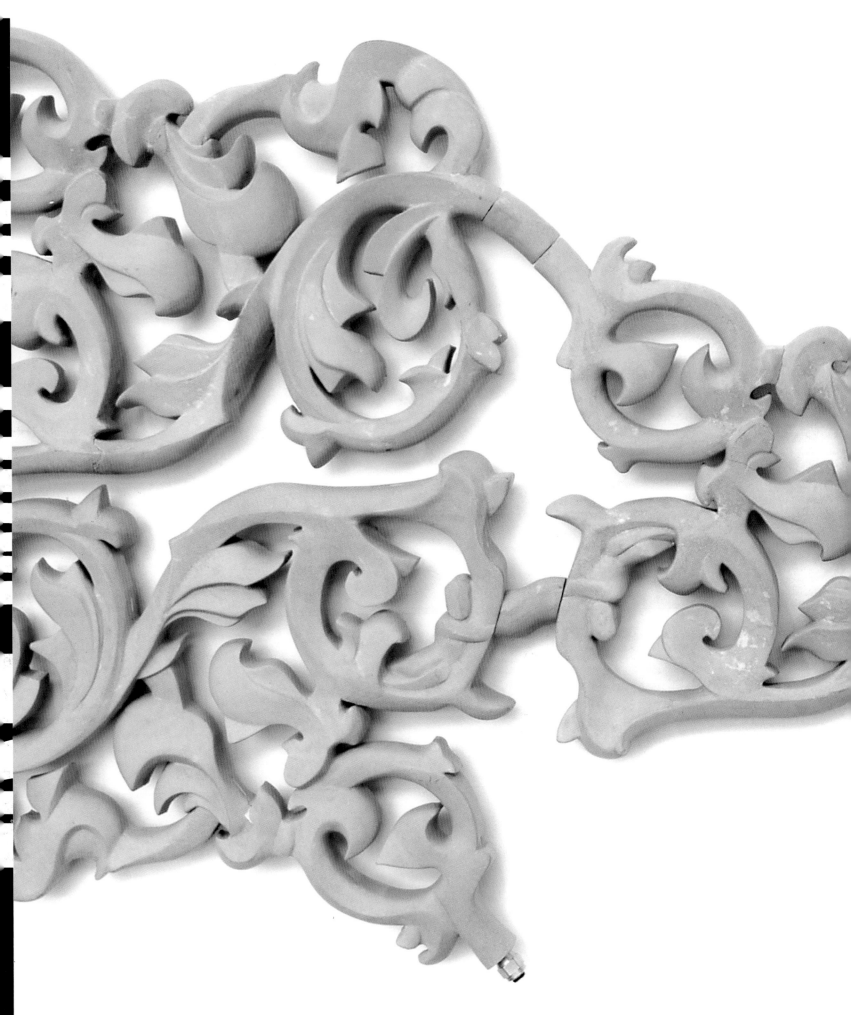

Product   Radiator
Designer   Joris Laarman
Materials   Concrete, plumbing parts
Dimensions   H: 65 x W: 250 x D: 45cm (25 ⅝ x 98 x 17 ¾in)
Manufacturer   Prototype, Droog Design, The Netherlands
Website   www.droogdesign.nl

Product   Alarm clock and weather station, The Starck Collection
Designer   Philippe Starck
Materials   Plastic, aluminium, LCD screen
Dimensions   Various sizes
Manufacturer   Oregon Scientific, France
Website   www.oregonscientific.fr

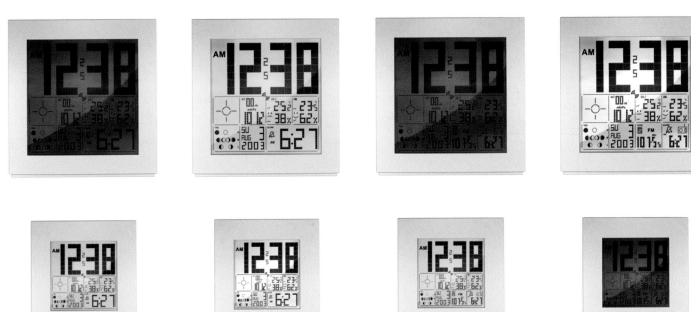

Product	Containers, Transparent Cakes
Designer	RADI Designers (R. Stadler, L. Massaloux, O. Sidet)
Materials	Blown/moulded glass
Dimensions	Various sizes
Manufacturer	Prototype, Canividro, Portugal
Website	www.radidesigners.com

The design world went food mad in 2004. A major proportion of the Milan Furniture Fair, both in and out of the exhibition ground, was devoted to dining. Furniture, in fact, seemed of secondary importance to the experience of eating and drinking. As well as minor exhibits that showcased biscuits (see Paolo Ulian's 'Finger Biscuit', page 36, and the Azumi's 'Spoon Biscuit', page 123, both for the Poppillan Free University of Bolzano show) and cake design by selected groups of invited international designers, both Cosmit (the organizers of the Salone) and *Interni* (Italy's leading magazine on

interiors and design) presented complementary dining experiences. On the fairground, Cosmit organized design schools from around the world to create a 'street' of differently designed restaurants, while at the Triennale, *Interni* commissioned a gastronomic journey through a series of street-dining venues from Marco Piva's pizza stand to Future Systems' water bar. Even Droog got on the bandwagon. Their 12th presentation at Milan was based on the concept of 'going slow'. Visitors watched as a group of elderly people prepared and served food and drinks to anyone who would pay for the experience.

RADI, therefore, are not alone in taking inspiration from the culinary. Their glassware series 'Transparent Cakes' was produced by blowing glass into various cake moulds, such as the Gugelhupf or a typical pie mould, in order to obtain different vessels. The bases of these tableware objects retain the imprint of the mould, while the shapes arising from the tin are freer and define the different types of uses from carafe to plate to vase.

Product   Chair, Mogu Missoni Balloon Chair
Designer   Yoshinobu Ishida
Materials   Lycra stretch filled with micro polystyrene balls covered
               with Missoni fabric
Dimensions   Diam. 70 x H. 70cm (27 ½ x 27 ½in)
Manufacturer   Prototype, Ebisukasei, Japan

In 2003 the Japanese Mogu phenomenon hit Milan. Design aficionados walked from show to show clutching brightly coloured and ultra-tactile 'playthings' that, irresistible as they were, they had pilfered from the Mogu exhibition. These anthropomorphic toys, filled with thousands of 0.5mm-diameter powder-beads, which gives them their fluid-like feel, became the 'must-have' Milan accessory. To touch was to be seduced.

During the Milan Design Week 2004 this industrial by-product came of age. The brainchild of Yoshinobu Ishida, whose parents own a plastic factory in Osaka, these minuscule polystyrene balls have now revolutionized the Japanese home-furnishing market. A major multimedia installation driven by touch presented Mogu's new collection, showing the potential of the material in a series of cushions, pillows, stuffed toys and furniture designed by leading international designers.

Product	Modular table system, coffee table, Grid
Designer	Nuf design, Inc. (Yeonsoo Son, Yoyo Wong,
	Kuni Jimbo, Kaori Ito)
Materials	Powder-coated sheet aluminium
Dimensions	H: 45.7 x W: 95.3 x D: 47.6cm (18 x 37 ½ x 18 ¾in)
Manufacturer	Nuf design, Inc, USA
Website	www.nufdesign.com

Product	Case goods, Kabuki
Designer	Kenneth Cobonpue
Materials	MDF, stainless steel
Dimensions	H: 130 x W: 70 x D: 40cm (51 x 27 ½ x 15 ¾in)
Manufacturer	Interior Crafts of the Islands, Inc, The Philippines
Website	www.kennethcobonpue.com

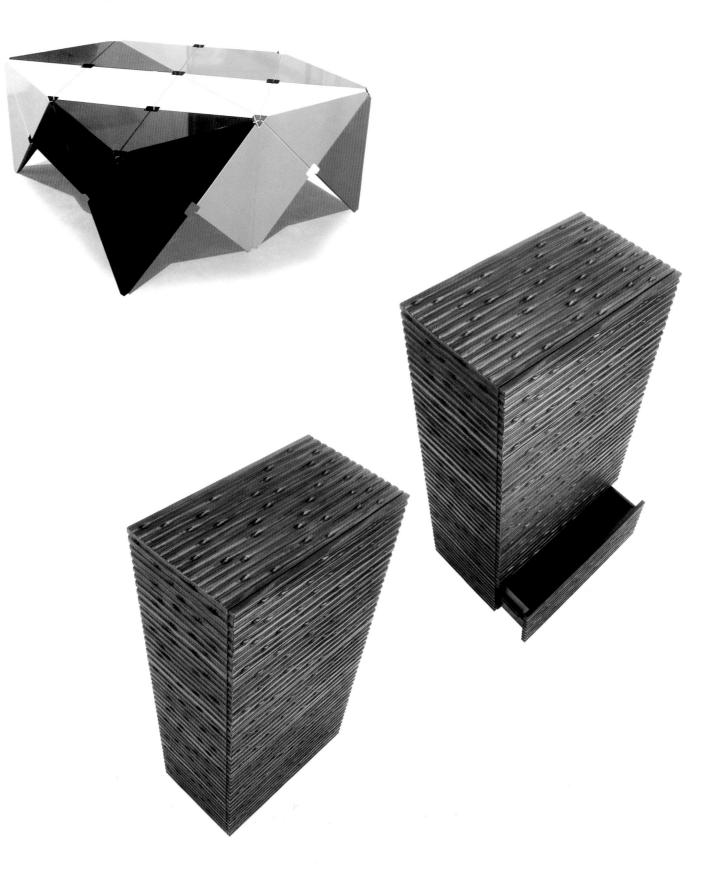

Product   Lounge chair, Paloma
Designer   Kenneth Cobonpue
Materials   Rattan, nylon wire
Dimensions   H: 61 x W: 130 x D: 96.5cm (24 x 51 x 38in)
Manufacturer Interior Crafts of the Islands, Inc, The Philippines
Website   www.kennethcobonpue.com

Kenneth Cobonpue first made his name at the Milan Furniture Fair 2001 when he showed his work alongside other designers from the Philippines in a joint show called Movement 8. Describing his design philosophy at that time he told me that he looked at nature with the purity and innocence of a child finding in it perfect visual qualities that were waiting to be transformed into modern man-made objects. Since then he has continued to use natural materials in unexpected and innovative ways, combining traditional skills with modern technology.

The 'Paloma' lounge chair uses thick rattan strips that have been steamed and bent over a structural rattan frame, each individually tied with nylon wire. This manufacturing process, developed by Cobonpue, is faster, easier and more cost efficient than the customary bentwood technique.

A departure from the majority of his products, which use bamboo and rattan indigenous to his country, 'Kabuki' (see page 119) is constructed from MDF. This fabricated material has been hand crafted: special tools are used to incise a pattern that imitates embedded bamboo stalks and the surface is then hand-rubbed and polished four times with three different layers of colour. The name 'Kabuki' is the word for a traditional form of Japanese theatre.

Product   Public seating and plant pot, Land Ho!
Designer   Rosario Hurtado and Roberto Feo, El Ultimo Grito
Materials   Roto-moulded polypropylene
Dimensions   H: 80 x Diam: 150cm (31 x 59in)
Manufacturer Nola Industrier AB, Sweden
Website   www.elultimogrito.co.uk

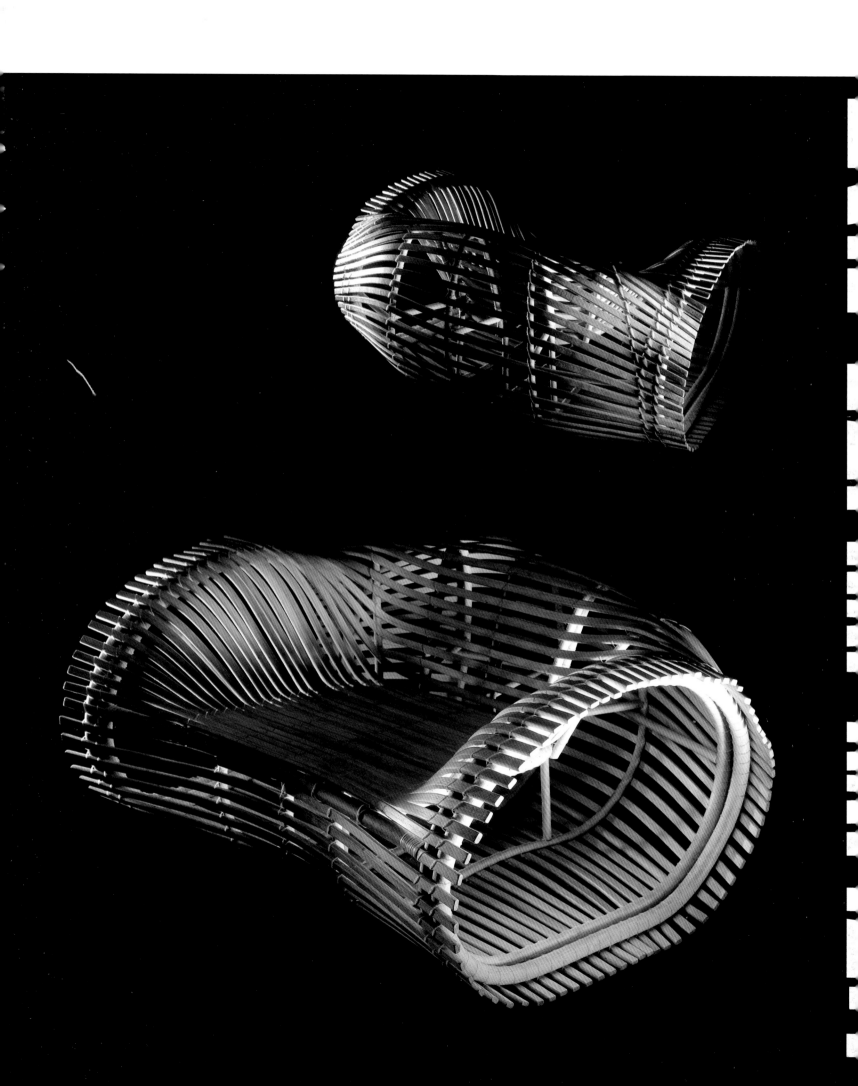

Product	Disposable mobile phone, 001.007
Designer	Chris Christou, Youmeus Design Ltd
Materials	Recycled paper pulp
Dimensions	H: 11 x W: 3.5 x D: 1.8cm (4 ⅜ x 1 ⅜ x ¾in)
Manufacturer	Prototype, Chris Christou, Youmeus Design Ltd, UK
Website	www.youmeusdesign.com

How come the most beautiful is disposable?
Maarten Baas

Product	Biscuit, Spoon Biscuit
Designer	Shin & Tomoko Azumi
Materials	Flour, butter, sugar, honey, milk, cocoa, chocolate
Dimensions	H: 1.1 x W: 2.3 x L: 11.3cm (⅜ x 1 x 4 ½in)
Manufacturer	One-off, Shin & Tomoko Azumi, UK
Website	www.azumi.co.uk

In spite of dessertspoons, tablespoons and egg spoons, the teaspoon continued to be a spoon. In spite of sugar lumps and dispensers, the teaspoon continued to be a spoon. In spite of the fact that it is now a cookie, the teaspoon continues to be a spoon. There aren't many objects this self-willed!

Maarten Baas

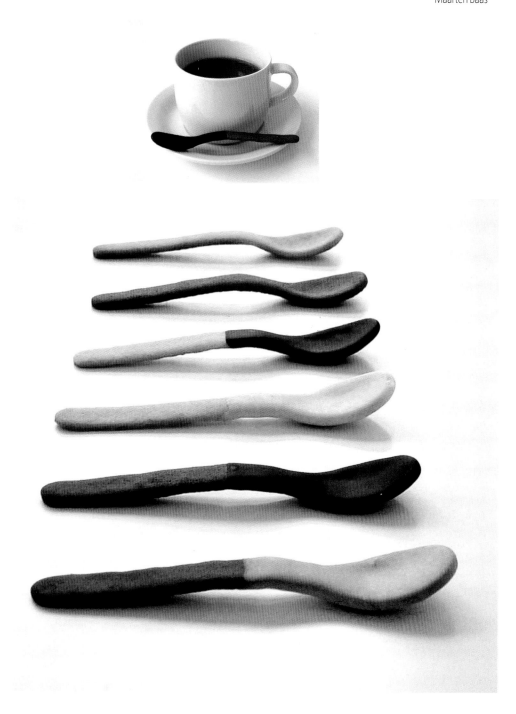

Product   Entertainment robot, Aibo ERS-7
Designer   Yuka Takeda, Daisuke Ishii, Taku Sugawara,
               Jun Uchiyama
Materials   ABS, vegetable-based plastic, silicone
Dimensions   H: 27.8 x W: 18 x D: 31.9cm (11 x 7 ⅛ x 12 ⅝in)
Manufacturer   Sony Corporation, Japan
Website   www.sony.co.jp

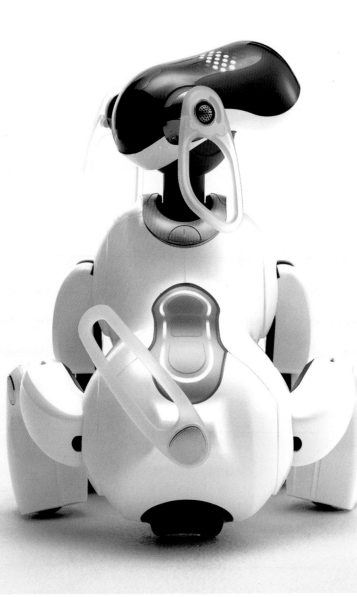

Rather like a prostitute, Aibo ERS-7 may greet you at your door with pre-programmed messages of welcome, it may cavort for pleasure with its many toys and will even preen under the caresses of your hand, but it will never love you. Fine as a family 'pet' or child's plaything, it's a rather negative comment on our highly technological, hectic city (but ultimately rather lonely and alienating twentyfirst-century) existence that Sony describe their latest interactive robot in the following words: 'AIBO can see, hear, feel for itself and walk. ... Through sharing your memories, learning your likes, getting to know your environment, AIBO will become in every way a truly unique individual. Entertaining and comforting you when you're glad, sad or angry. Reflecting a wide range of emotions through its uniquely LED-guided face, AIBO will become, in fact, your best friend.'

Aibo's 'character' is contained within its many cutting-edge software programs. It expresses itself through LEDs – blue for happy, red for angry – and lifelike body language. AIBO 'sees' thanks to a colour vision camera mounted above its mouth. Equipped with face recognition technology, the little robot will 'remember' your face and distinguish you from strangers. Infrared distance sensors next to the camera and on the main body help AIBO avoid obstacles and walk around your home. Your 'pet' feels through electric-static sensors on the crown of its head and will react to your strokes. Sensors on each paw means that AIBO will walk differently on different surfaces – it will even lift a paw to shake your hand. The chin is sensitive too, as is its back: stroke it and it will respond with its happy blue lights, tap it and its eyes will glow red. Stereo microphones mounted on either side help your little doggy listen and interact with you and it will turn toward you when you issue a voice command. The centrepiece of AIBO's artificial intelligence is the 'MIND' software, located on a removable memory stick, which controls all behaviour as well as the applications that connect wirelessly with your PC or mobile. In short, there is little AIBO can't do for you. It will take pictures either by transmitted command, or (more disturbingly) of its own accord, send e-mails and play back recorded messages to your family. It will reflect your own body rhythms and wake up and fall asleep when you do. It can locate its energy station and recharge without your help. It will entertain you with music and acrobatics and express its feeling with amusing sounds. What it won't do, however, is die for you, which of course is what we expect from Man's best friend. AIBO is more likely to dance on your grave.

Product	Table and console, Keramic table
Designer	Bruno Fattorini
Materials	Matt-lacquered aluminium, laminated porcelain
Dimensions	Various sizes
Manufacturer	MDF Italia, Italy
Website	www.mdfitalia.it

Product   Stackable chair, Lac
Designer   Jasper Morrison
Materials   Polypropylene, leather
Dimensions   W: 49 x D: 51 x H: 77.5cm (19 ¼ x 20 ⅛ x 31in)
Manufacturer Cap Design SpA, Italy
Website   www.cappellini.it

Product   Chair, Network
Designer   Archirivolto
Materials   Fibreglass-reinforced techno-polymer,
             plastic mesh/steel webbing
Dimensions   H: 76.5 x W: 50.5 x D: 51.5cm (30 x 20 ⅛ x 20 ½in)
Manufacturer Segis SpA, Italy
Website   www.segis.it

Product   Textile, Repeat Classic Print (detail)
Designer   Hella Jongerius
Materials   Cotton, rayon, polyester
Dimensions   W: 140cm (55in)
Manufacturer   Maharam, USA
Website   www.jongeriuslab.com
               www.maharam.com

Product	Multi-sensory audiovisual sofa, Music Image Sofa System (M.I.S.S.)
Designer	Philippe Starck
Materials	Can be upholstered in fabric, feather or polyester filling, lacquered wood, special technical fabric permeable to sound and infrared rays of the remote control
Dimensions	L: 216–294cm x D: 107–123cm (85–116 x 42–48in)
Manufacturer	Cassina SpA, Italy
Website	www.cassina.it

The 'Music Image Sofa System' ('M.I.S.S.') is the final outcome of years of research and collaboration between Starck and Cassina into developing new furniture typologies to suit the evolving patterns of the way we live and function within our home environments. It's always difficult to invent new ideas for comparatively uncomplicated forms such as beds and settees, yet Starck's concept is completely fresh, fusing as it does domestic technology and furnishing. This is a sofa that houses a hi-fi integrated for home theatre and planned to function with any make of appliance. The external appearance is void of any reference to what is contained within – Starck refers to 'the minimum in the maximum'. The system is made up of two parts: the sofa itself and a 'totem', which houses certain appliances and a screen. The sofa contains the speakers, two set in either end of the back, and a sub-woofer, hidden in the inner part of the larger arm. Sounds come from within the upholstery as if by magic. A projector can be included and is hidden in a compartment behind the back of the sofa. The divan and the screen have to be set a certain distance from one another, and to conceal the micro-cables and micro-connections between the two, Starck has developed an integral 'carpet'. To complement the design, Starck has also created M.I.S.T.E.R., an accompanying settee in various measurements and arrangements but without the technical content.

Product	Table with two levels, Libellule
Designer	Bernard Vuarnesson
Materials	Wood, stainless steel
Dimensions	H: 40 / 73 x W: 85 x L: 146 / 211cm
	(15 ¾ / 28 ¾ x 33 x 57 / 83in)
Manufacturer	One-off, Bellato Pallucco, Italy
Website	www.vuarnesson.com

Product	Computer peripherals/networking box
	(for the home), Netgear Platinum II
Designer	Newdealdesign LLC. (Gadi Amit, Yoshi Hoshino,
	Bryan Grziwok, Mike Massucco)
Materials	Injection-moulded ABS, mylar label
Dimensions	H: 17.2 x W: 11.4 x D: 2.7cm (6 ¾ x 4 ½ x 1in)
Manufacturer	Netgear Inc, USA
Website	www.newdealdesign.com

Computer accessories are often boring and utilitarian in design. The Netgear Platinum II communication box, which houses a Wi-Fi board, is anything but. Sitting alongside the home PC or entertainment system, it is understated but, unlike the usual bland boxes, draws attention to itself by a clever use of light and material. The exterior band has two layers: the inner of a mirror material and the exterior made from clear plastic in the shape of a lens. The combination of these two layers creates an optical effect. The housing reflects the colour and textures of the surroundings while the mirror projects a band of light around the perimeter of the product, an effect that contrasts with the generic shadow found around similar products. The stand, which enables the box to be used vertically as well as horizontally, lends a quirky, almost cartoon effect to this little box.

Product   Celadon porcelain plates, Relief
Designer   Masatoshi Sakaegi
Materials   Porcelain
Dimensions   Various sizes
Manufacturer   Sakaegi Design Studio, Japan

Product	Wallpaper, Cornici
Designer	Jordi Pigem de Palol and Enrico Azzimonti
Materials	Paper
Dimensions	W: 60 x L: 300cm (23 ⅝ x 118in)
Manufacturer	Prototype, Jordi Pigem de Palol and
	Enrico Azzimonti
Website	www.enricoazzimonti.it

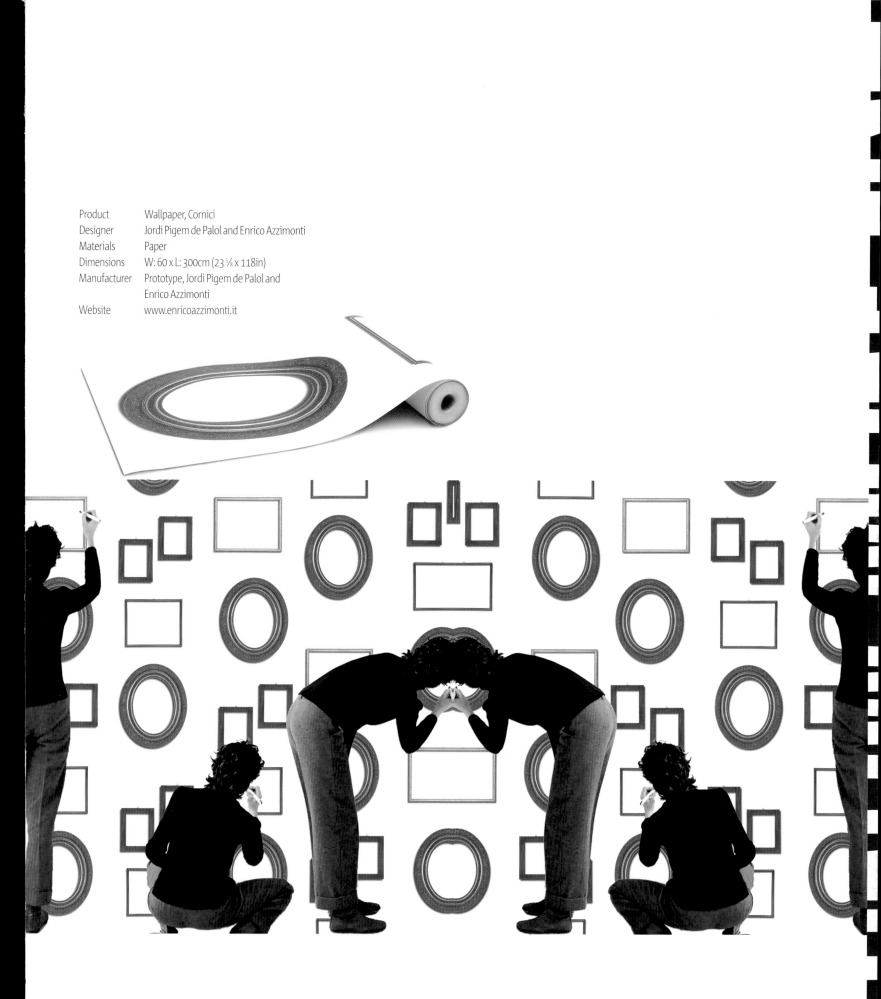

Product   Ceiling lamp, Alquimista
Designer   Robert Stadler
Materials   Textiles, E27 globe light bulb
Dimensions   H: 75 x Diam: 65cm (29 ½ x 25 ⅝in)
Manufacturer One-off, Coopa Roca, Brazil
Website   www.robertstadler.net

Product   Underwear packaging, Devo
Designer   Yves Béhar, Fuseproject
Materials   Biodegradable cornstarch
Dimensions   H: 31.8 x W: 21.6cm (12 ½ x 8 ½in)
Manufacturer Prototype, Yves Béhar, Fuseproject
Website   www.fuseproject.com

The ultimate in biodegradable packaging, Yves Béhar's underwear container for Devo is produced in cornstarch and dissolves in water.

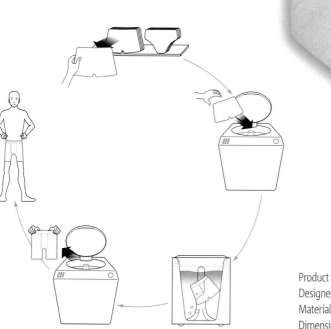

Product   Surface pattern, 61 Mixed Posy 7
Designer   Debbie Jane Buchan
Materials   Not applicable
Dimensions   H: 14 x W: 12cm (5 ½ x 4 ¾in)
Manufacturer One-off, Debbie Jane Buchan, UK

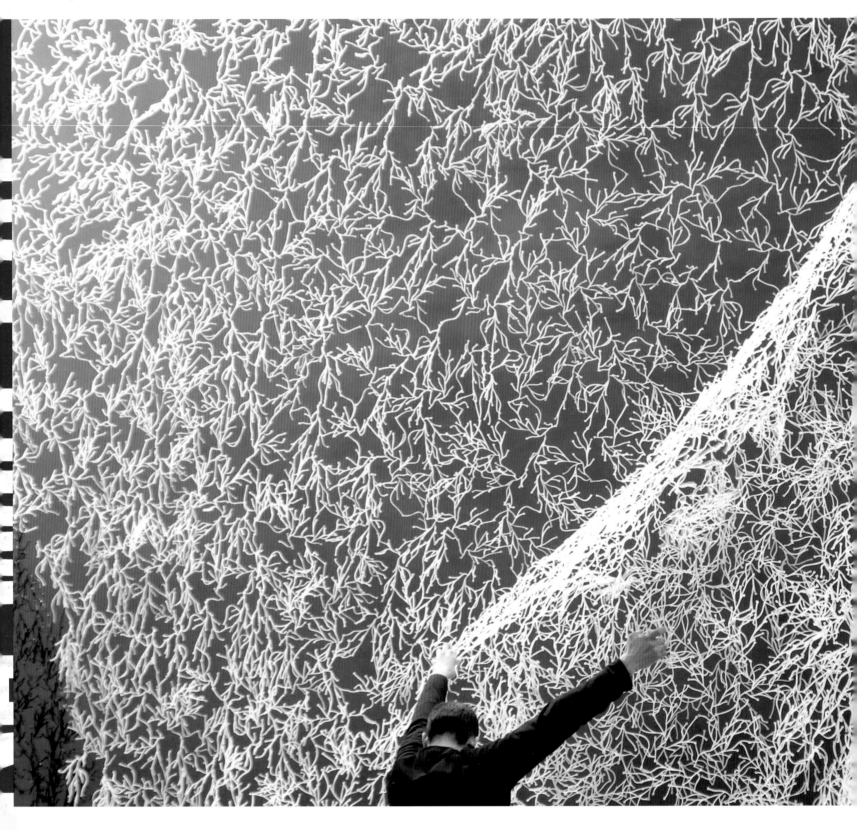

*Alltough it seems a terrible job to actually connect all the elements, the
result makes you instantly forget this and leads your mind beyond its play-
mobile-like appearance straight into the wondrous wavy, oceanic
kelpwoods. This product has a serious 'I want it' feeling!*
Chris Kabel

Less is more, more is better! Very poetic mass-production.
Wieki Somers

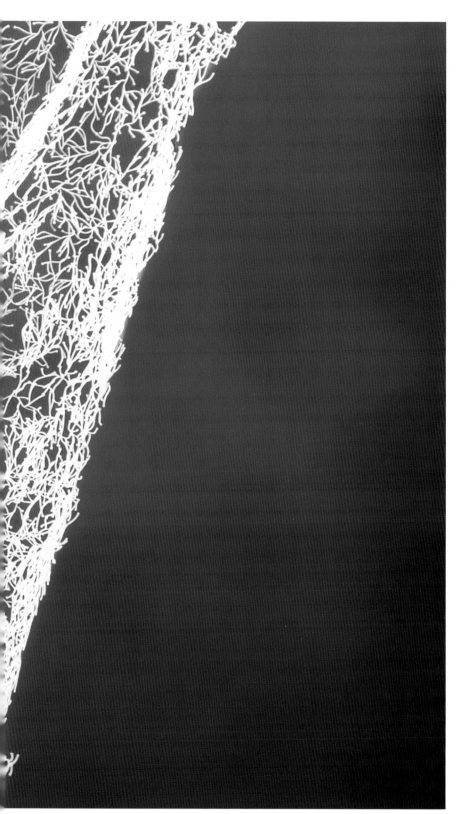

Product   Modular clipping system, Algue
Designer   Ronan and Erwan Bouroullec
Materials   Injected ABS
Dimensions   (Module) 27 x 23 x 4cm (10 ⅝ x 9 x 1 ⅝in)
Manufacturer   Vitra, Switzerland
Website   www.vitra.com

IMM Cologne is the main showcase venue for furniture design from Northern Europe. Due to the unfavourable economic situation in Germany, linked with the increase in importance of such regional fairs as 'Maison et Objet' in Paris, the 'Stockholm Furniture Fair', and 'Interieur' in Kortrijk, Belgium, this show has become progressively less exciting, with many major manufacturers now not bothering to reserve stands. This year, for example, there was little representation from Sweden, France's XO chose to stay away and Italy's Cassina SpA, which normally previews its new designs in Cologne rather than Milan, showed in Paris instead. One feature that is worth making the trip to Germany in January to see, however, is the ideal house installation. It was instigated in 2003, when Karim Rashid and Konstantin Grcic were invited to come up with their concept for the perfect living space, and in 2004 it was the turn of the Campana and Bouroullec brothers.

Both groups were in agreement that the idea of the perfect home is a very subjective one and as such should not be dictated. There is no ultimate solution and the results of their deliberations showed two very different realities. The Bouroullec's house was a jigsaw puzzle of interlocking walls, which can be constructed and deconstructed following the various life changes of the inhabitants. They have suggested basic components that can be easily adapted, clicking into place without tools, and have used industrially produced materials, adapting technology to create a natural effect. When first approached to conceive their ideal home, Ronan and Erwan Bouroullec were reluctant to participate, considering that to have one designer create everything in an environment was a bad idea. However, they used the opportunity to test a new product concept: a small plastic branched clipping device that can be 'knitted' together like a textile to act as a room divider or screen.

The first prototype was produced for a French advertising agency BETC, who used it to create a rooftop sun pavilion. At this stage the 'clip' was angular, resembling a clothes peg. For the ideal home installation, this had evolved into an organic module, each creeping and joining the next like the spores of moss or algae, creating verdant walls. The plastic-clip system, 'Algue', is now part of Vitra's launch of residential products, which includes other pieces by the brothers and by Jasper Morrison. Commenting on the Bouroullecs, and the clip in particular, Rolf Fehlbaum, the Chief Executive of Vitra, writes 'Their work makes you wonder, "How did someone come up with that idea? It's so odd, why would you do that?" It's work that emerges not in the spirit of necessity, but which opens a new poetic possibility. It makes you think, "Yes, why not?"'

Product   Shoes, Birkenstock Birkis and clip
Designer   Yves Béhar, Fuseproject
Materials   Biodegradable TPU, EVA
Dimensions   H: 10.8 x W: 15.9 x L: 33cm (4 ¼ x 6 ¼ x 13in)
Manufacturer Birkenstock, USA
Website   www.fuseproject.com

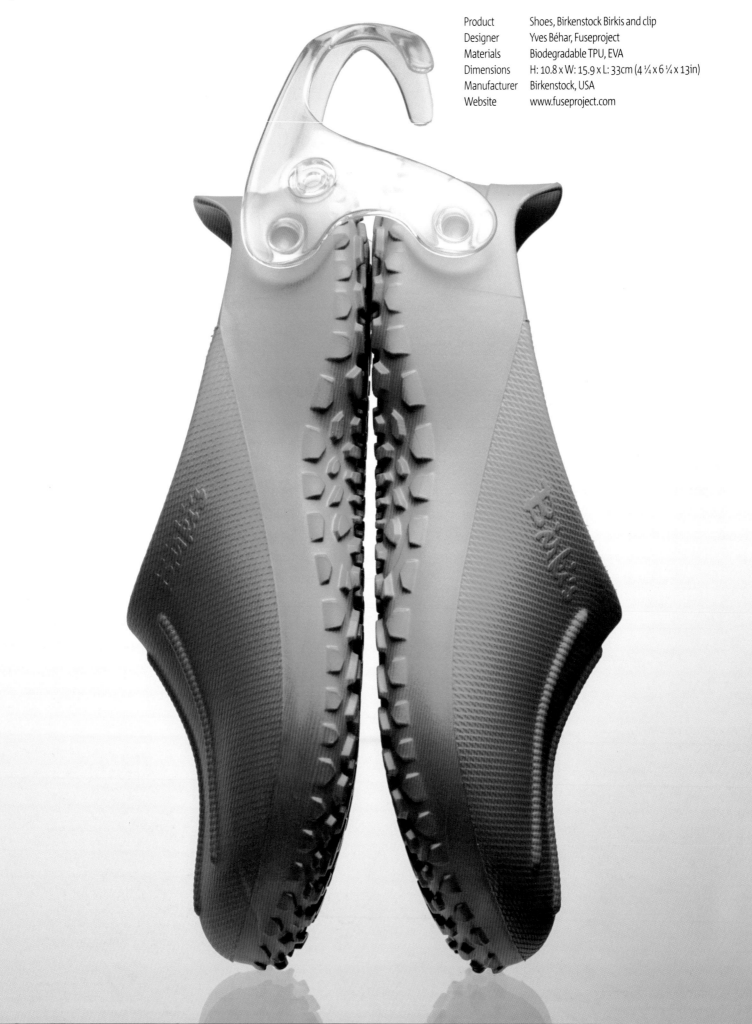

Product   Chair, Nais
Designer   Alfredo Häberli
Materials   Chromium-plated or colour-coated steel, removable cover
              in canvas, fabric or leather, lightly quilted
Dimensions   H: 82cm / (seat) 46cm x W: (with armrests) 56cm
              (without armrests) 46cm x D: 53cm
              (32 ¼ / 18 ⅛ x 22 / 18 ⅛ x 20 ⅞in)
Manufacturer ClassiCon GmbH, Germany
Website   www.classicon.com

Product   Long board, The Equilibrist
Designer   Weyers & Borms
Materials   Polyurethane covered with glassfibre-reinforced polyester
Dimensions   H: 13 x W: 17 x L: 360cm (5 ⅛ x 6 ¾ x 142in)
Manufacturer Limited batch production, Weyers & Borms, Belgium

Product	Lighting, Leonardo
Designer	Antoni Arola
Materials	Maple wood strips, steel cubic-shaped shell; light source: incandescent E-27/150W bulb
Dimensions	Diam: 60 / 120cm (23 ⅝ / 47in)
Manufacturer	Santa & Cole, SA, Spain
Website	www.estudiarola.com

Product   Bench, Volta
Designer   Shin & Tomoko Azumi
Materials   Three-dimensional bent plywood
Dimensions   H: 43 x W: 120 x D: 40cm (16 ⅞ x 47 x 15 ¾in)
Manufacturer Lapalma, Italy
Website   www.azumi.co.uk

Product   Textile, Repeat (elements)
Designer   Hella Jongerius
Materials   Cotton, rayon, polyester
Dimensions   W: 140cm (55in)
Manufacturer Maharam, USA
Websites   www.jongeriuslab.com
             www.maharam.com

Product   Outdoor lamp (for swimming pools), Waterproof
Designer   Héctor Serrano
Materials   Rotation-moulded polyethylene; light source: E-10 4.8V
             0.75A (waterproof and rechargeable) light bulb
Dimensions   H: 53 x W: 23cm (20 ⅞ x 9in)
Manufacturer Metalarte, Spain
Website   www.metalarte.com

Product   Surface pattern, 66 Mixed Posy 12
Designer   Debbie Jane Buchan
Materials   Not applicable
Dimensions   H: 14 x W: 12cm (5 ½ x 4 ¾in)
Manufacturer Prototype, Debbie Jane Buchan, UK

Product   Surface pattern, 81 Hidden heart
Designer   Debbie Jane Buchan
Materials   Not applicable
Dimensions   H: 22 x W: 23cm (8 ⅝ x 9in)
Manufacturer One-off, Debbie Jane Buchan, UK

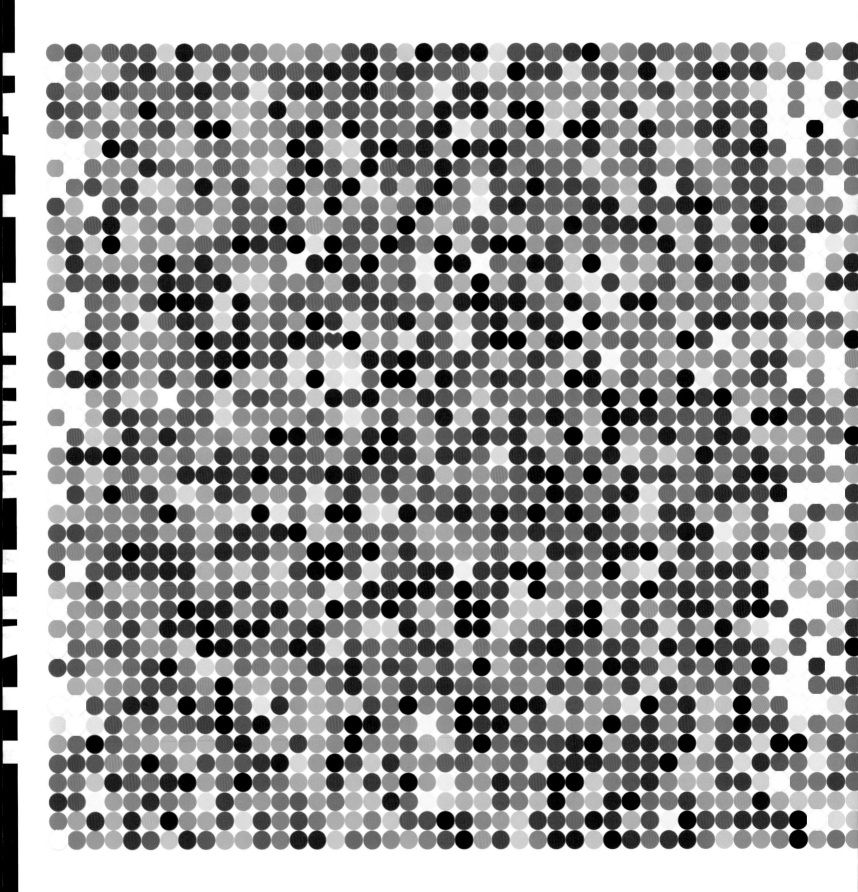

Product   Mobile phone, Talby
Designer   Marc Newson
Materials   Aluminium, plastic
Dimensions   W: 4.4 x H: 12.4 x D: 1cm (1 ¾ x 4 ⅞ x ⅜in)
Manufacturer   Prototype, KDDI Corporation, Japan
Website   www.marc-newson.com

Product   Choir stall for Portsmouth Cathedral, UK
Designer   Edward Barber and Jay Osgerby, Barber Osgerby
Materials   Solid oak
Dimensions   H: 69 x W: 110 x D: 43 (27 ⅛ x 43 x 16 ⅞in)
Manufacturer Limited batch production, Isokon Plus, UK
Website   www.barberosgerby.com

Product	Textile, Repeat Classic Print (detail)
Designer	Hella Jongerius
Materials	Cotton, rayon, polyester
Dimensions	W: 140cm (55in)
Manufacturer	Maharam, USA
Website	www.jongeriuslab.com
	www.maharam.com

Product	Armchair, Girotondo
Designer	Alessandro Mendini
Materials	Structure in steel with variable-density polyurethane filler, covered with polyester batting, steel legs with filler in polyurethane foam, rubber feet, cover in fabric or leather
Dimensions	H: 100 (seat: 43) x W: 73 x D: 86cm (16 ⅞/ 39 x 28 ¾ x 34in)
Manufacturer	De Padova, Italy
Website	www.ateliermendini.it www.depadova.it

Product   Luxury Heineken bottle
Designer   Ora-Ïto
Materials   Brushed aluminium
Dimensions   H: 18cm (7 ⅛in)
Manufacturer   Heineken, The Netherlands
Website   www.ora-ito.com

Product   Surface pattern, 58 Mixed Posy 4
Designer   Debbie Jane Buchan
Materials   Not applicable
Dimensions   H: 14 x W: 12cm (5 ½ x 4 ¾in)
Manufacturer   Prototype, Debbie Jane Buchan, UK

Product	Four-door/four-wheel drive car, Porsche Cayenne
Designer	Harm Lagaay (Head of Design) and
	Stephen Murkett (Project Leader)
Materials	Steel
Dimensions	L: 478.2 x W (inc mirrors): 221.6 x H: 169.9cm (188 x 87 x 67in)
Manufacturer	Porsche AG, Germany
Website	www.porsche.com

Product   Textile, Kirie 2004
Designer   Yoshiki Hishinuma
Materials   100% Polyester
Dimensions   50 x 50cm (19 ⅝ x 19 ⅝in)
Manufacturer Limited batch production,
              Yoshiki Hishinuma Co. Ltd, Japan
Website   www.yoshikihishinuma.co.jp

Product	Chair, Flo chair (red)	Product	Bar stool, Mart (white)
Designer	Patricia Urquiola	Designer	Roderick Vos
Materials	Steel, rattan	Materials	Chromed steel, polyethylene
Dimensions	H: 86 (seat: 45) x W: 53 x D: 53cm	Dimensions	H: 115 (seat: 82) x W: 41 x D: 59cm
	(34 / 17 ¾ x 20 ⅞ x 20 ⅞in)		(45 / 32 x 16 ⅛ x 23 ¼in)
Manufacturer	Driade, SpA, Italy	Manufacturer	Driade, SpA, Italy
Website	www.driade.com	Website	www.driade.com

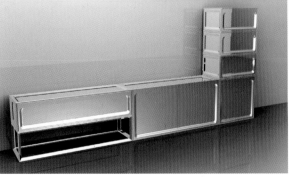

Product   Modular storage system, Progetto Tom Box
Designer   Tom Dixon
Materials   Steel, plastic, MDF
Dimensions   Various sizes
Manufacturer   Pallucco, Italy
Website   www.pallucco.com

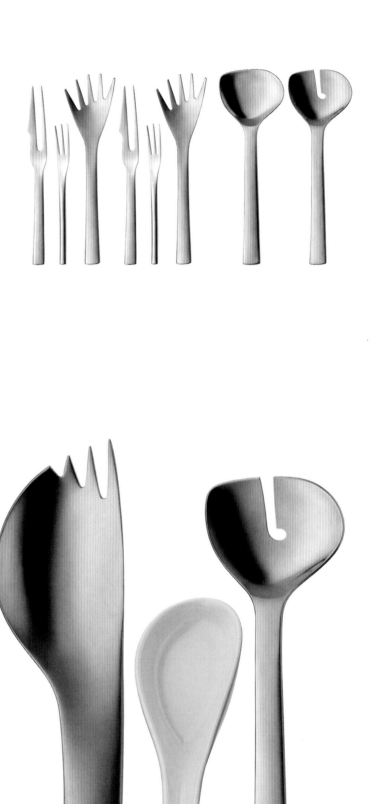

*Don't know if they all work well, but they're so
beautiful that I don't care!*
Ineke Hans

Product	Speciality cutlery, Style
Designer	Daniel Eltner
Materials	Cromargan® (stainless steel 18110), premium wood, porcelain
Dimensions	Various sizes
Manufacturer	WMF Aktiengesellschaft, Germany
Website	www.wmf.de

A quirky take on the post-modern dictum 'form follows function', each piece of Daniel Eltner's cutlery range, 'Style', is created to be used only with certain food types. All share a thick and sculpturally simple chunky aesthetic, which makes them easy to use. Eltner considered not only the form of the human body but also table ritual and cultural pointers before developing each ergonomically conceived item. The pasta server, for example, is an extension of the outstretched arm, with the head deliberately asymmetrical to mimic the human hand, and the pasta is gripped by wide-spread 'fingers'. The knife-spoon-fork was designed for the Oriental set. Observing that it is all but impossible to cut the meatball in wan-tang soup with the porcelain spoon usually provided, Eltner worked on a new material, which blends Cromargan and porcelain to produce a keener edge. The dumpling is dissected and can then either be skewered or cupped. The porcelain bowl is drop-formed to integrate the handle of the spoon-fork.

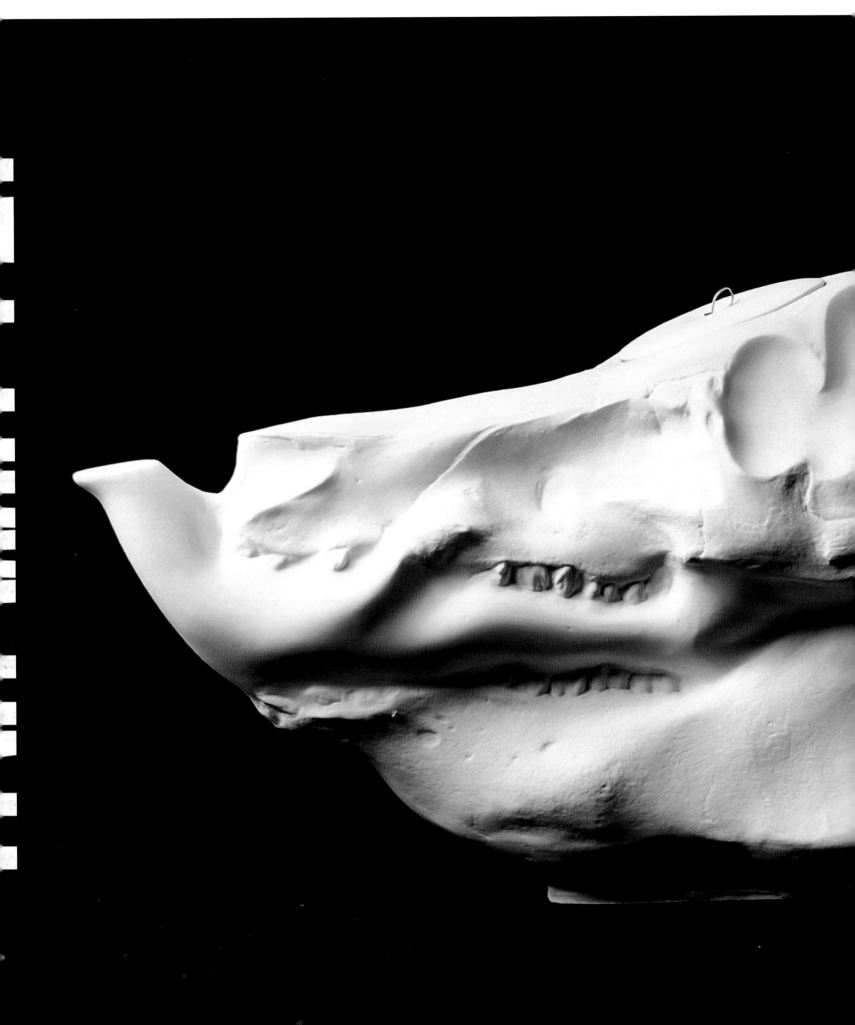

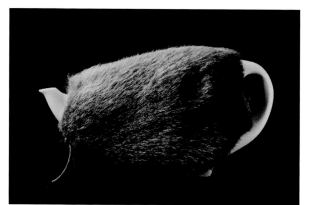

Product	Teapot, High Teapot (Deliciously Decadent!)
Designer	Wieki Somers
Materials	Bone China (porcelain), fur (water rat), stainless steel, leather
Dimensions	L: 47 x W: 20 x H: 25cm (18 ½ x 7 ⅞ x 9 ⅞in)
Manufacturer	Limited batch production, European Ceramic Work Centre, The Netherlands
Website	www.wiekisomers.com

If any modern movement is associated with liberating dark feelings, surely it is Surrealism. Many have felt particularly threatened by one of its anxious objects, a fur-lined teacup, which became Meret Oppenheim's most famous work, and not solely because of its playfulness. It has suggested to many viewers that they must taste something bristly and inaccessible and that it alludes to female sexuality. This object was the first thing that sprang to my mind when I was confronted by the 'High Teapot' from Wieki Somers' 'Deliciously Decadent!' project. Nowhere is this reference made by the designer, yet the connection would suggest at least a sub-conscious motivation. I was interested to find out that the designer is female. She was trained at the Design Academy, Eindhoven, and then worked for Droog, so it's not surprising that many of her designs have a witticism about them and that they poetically investigate the characteristics and possibilities of materials. Somers describes the teapot and cover as a hunting trophy for the high-tea table, equating one example of decadency as the human need for status and superiority over nature through exploitation of animals. The tea cosy is made from water rat fur, while the teapot is produced in semi-transparent, snow-white porcelain containing bone (bone china). The tea is visible through the thin cast.

Product	Chair, Loop Chair (A 660)
Designer	James Irvine
Materials	Bentwood, aluminium, webbing
Dimensions	H: (seat) 46 x W: 51cm (18 ⅛ x 20 ⅛in)
Manufacturer	Thonet, Germany
Website	www.thonet.de

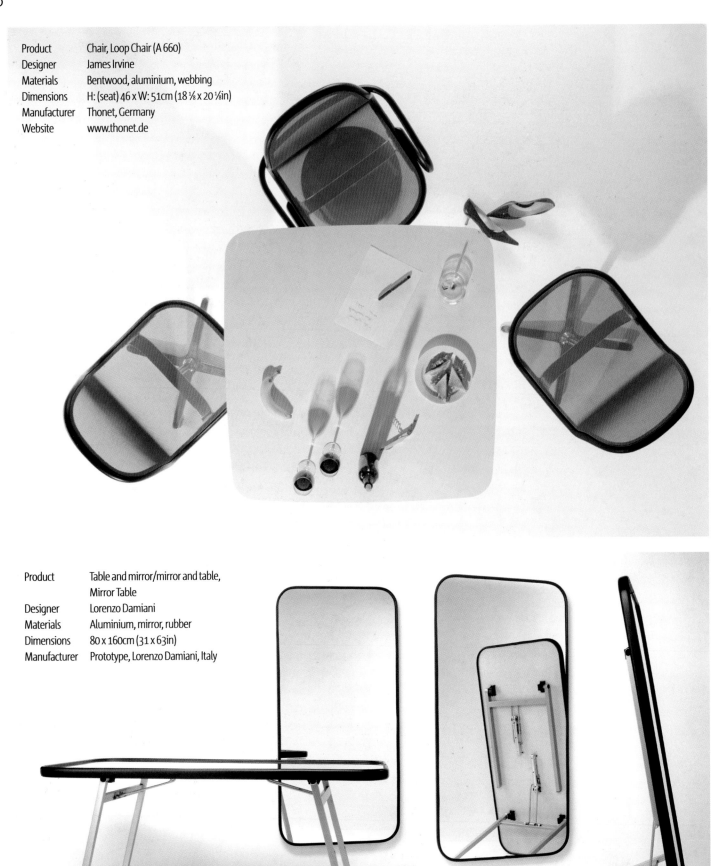

Product	Table and mirror/mirror and table,
	Mirror Table
Designer	Lorenzo Damiani
Materials	Aluminium, mirror, rubber
Dimensions	80 x 160cm (31 x 63in)
Manufacturer	Prototype, Lorenzo Damiani, Italy

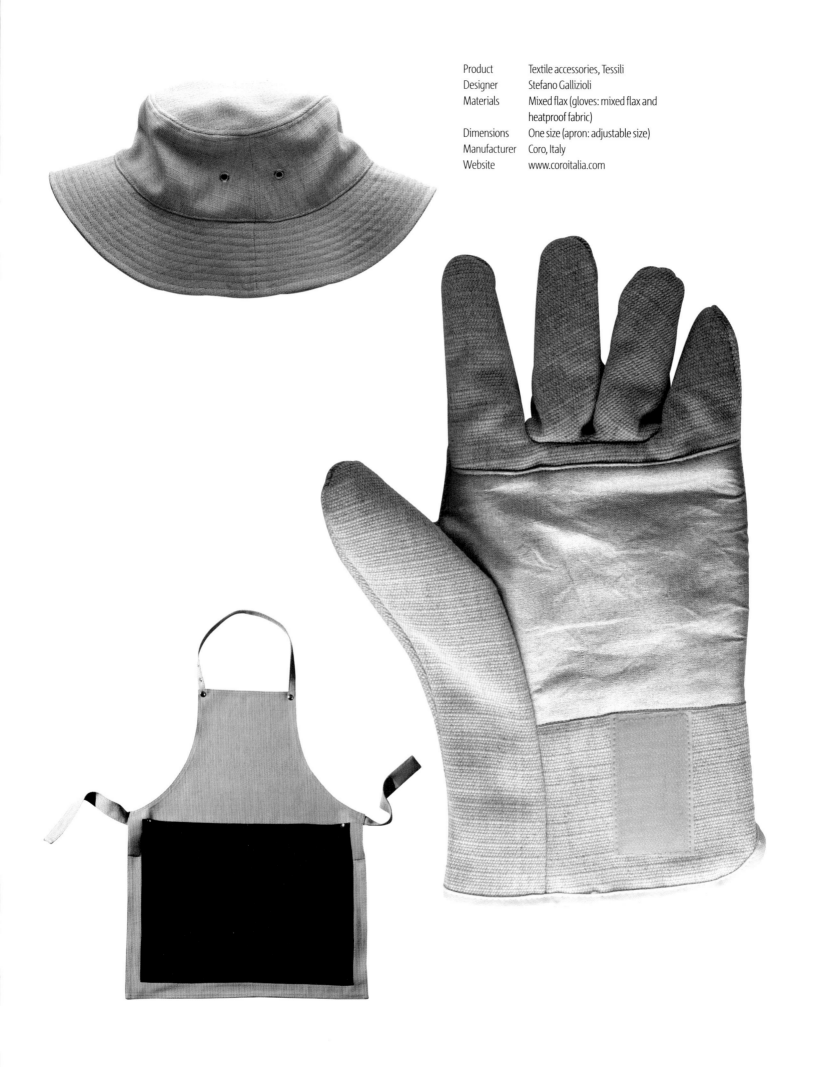

Product   Textile accessories, Tessili
Designer   Stefano Gallizioli
Materials   Mixed flax (gloves: mixed flax and
               heatproof fabric)
Dimensions   One size (apron: adjustable size)
Manufacturer   Coro, Italy
Website   www.coroitalia.com

Product	Tableware, Best of Snoopy (Flower Strip collection)
Designer	Michael Sieger, Sieger Design
Materials	Porcelain
Dimensions	Mug; 0.3L (10fl oz); bowl; 0.4L (14fl oz); cup and saucer: 0.25L (9fl oz); plate (Diam) 22cm (8 ⅝in)
Manufacturer	United Labels AG, Germany
Website	www.sieger-design.com

Product	Home entertainment device, Moviebeam receiver and remote
Designer	Yves Béhar, Fuseproject
Materials	Injected-moulded ABS
Dimensions	H: 11.4 x W: 30.5 x L: 30.5cm (4 ½ x 12 x 12in)
Manufacturer	Buenavista Datacasting, USA
Website	www.fuseproject.com

Although John R. Hoke III, Nike's Vice President and Global Creative Director of footwear design, recently referred to Yves Béhar as 'a fantastic design force ... [who's] about to explode onto the world scene', Béhar has actually been making his mark since the late '90s when he designed the distinctive and well-publicized accessories that surrounded the launch of the new Mini Cooper. Unlike most automobile logo-based items, Mini-Motion concentrated instead on products that could be owned by people with or without the car itself. Recently, however, Béhar's profile has risen to such an extent that last year he was honoured with a solo show at the San Francisco Museum of Modern Art, which he referred to as a 'Futurspective' rather than a 'Retrospective' (and for which, incidentally, he designed a smart shoe, complete with a chip that collected data on the wearer during their visit to the exhibition).

Yves Béhar, design principal and founder of Fuseproject, is a multidisciplinary industrial designer whose clients include Herman Miller, Nike, Birkenstock and Microsoft. He believes that his products should influence how design permeates culture; they should not only have lasting impact and be technologically sound, but should also communicate on a personal level with users, making them question the functioning of an object or why and how an item of clothing should be worn. If this connection is made, Beher argues, it can only be good for business, because the stronger and more complex the link with the consumer, the longer lasting customer loyalty will be. The opening message on his website is 'Design Brings Stories to Life' and his work is dedicated to creating narratives to develop our emotional experience of well-known brands. His most recent research is a non-product based investigation into consumers' perception of brands.

Béhar's 'Moviebeam' receiver and remote for Buenavista uses conventional FM signals to download, store and then play movies for a negligible monthly fee.

Product	Container/vase, Flower
Designer	Scholten & Baijings
Materials	Porcelain
Dimensions	9.5 x 12 x 12cm (3 ¾ x 4 ¾ x 4 ¾in)
Manufacturer	Produced within the framework of the European Ceramic Work Centre project, 'Dutch Souvenirs'
Website	www.scholtenbaijings.com

Part of the 'Dutch Souvenirs' series produced by the European Ceramic Work Centre, Scholten and Baijings 'Flower' container/vase is filled with the old Dutch liqueur 'Forget-Me-Not'. Distilled from flower buds, blossoms, brandy and rum, this long-life elixir has a distinctive floral aroma, which evokes the bygone era when the drink was given by womenfolk to their sailor husbands, or loved-ones, to be opened only when they reached their first port of call.

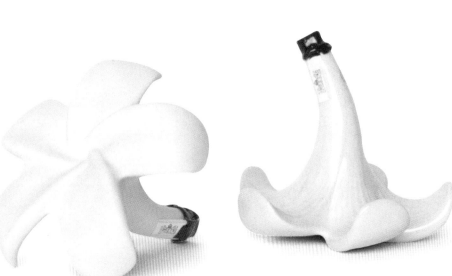

Product   'Architecture for flowers', Golden Gate (Blister Collection)
Designer   Andrea Branzi
Materials   Golden brass, enamelled metal, fine blown glass
Dimensions   72 x 18 x H: 25cm (28 ⅜ x 7 ⅛ x 9 ⅞in)
Manufacturer   Limited batch production, Design Gallery Milano, Italy
Website   www.designgallerymilano.com

Product   Kitchen system, Case system 2.3
Designer   Piero Lissoni
Materials   Pral®, stainless steel, graphite oak
Dimensions   Variable
Manufacturer   Boffi SpA, Italy
Website   www.boffi.com

Product	Fabric (new environmentally friendly upholstery), Waterborn
Designer	Jean Nouvel
Materials	55% polyurethane, 22.5% polyester, 22.5% nylon
Dimensions	W: 120cm (47in)
Manufacturer	Kvadrat, Denmark
Website	www.kvadrat.dk

Product	Small armchair, Dummy
Designer	Konstantin Grcic
Materials	Polyurethane foam, expanded polyethylene coupled with heat-sealed fabric
Dimensions	H: 81 (seat: 48) x D: 40 x W: 50 (32/18 ⅞ x 15 ¾ x 19 ⅝in)
Manufacturer	Moroso, Italy
Website	www.moroso.it

Product	Planter/vase/umbrella rack, Tall
Designer	Johannes Norlander
Materials	Polyurethane
Dimensions	H: 75cm x Diam. (top): 42/(base): 45cm (29 ½ x 16 ½/17 ¾in)
Manufacturer	Nola industrier AB, Sweden
Website	www.nola.se

The flexibility of rubber is used to great effect in Johannes Norlander's 'Tall'. By simply folding back the edges, the planter can be adapted for use as an umbrella stand.

Product	Armchair, Sponge
Designer	Peter Traag
Materials	Polyurethane, fluorocarbon polyester thread fabric
Dimensions	H: 75 x W: 85 x D: 94cm (29 ½ x 33 x 37in)
Manufacturer	Edra SpA, Italy
Website	www.edra.com

Product	Chair, Carbon Chair
Designer	Bertjan Pot and Marcel Wanders
Materials	Epoxy, carbon
Dimensions	H: 78 x W: 48 x D: 46cm (31 x 18 ⅞ x 18 ⅛in)
Manufacturer	Moooi, The Netherlands
Website	www.moooi.com

Bertjan Pot is a hero

Product	Tablecloth, Pantheon
Designer	Studio Job
Materials	Damask cotton/linen
Dimensions	W: 165 x L: 265cm (65 x 104in)
Manufacturer	Netherlands Textielmuseum, The Netherlands
Website	www.studiojob.be

Product   Eau de parfum bottle, Burberry Brit
Designer   Fabien Baron
Materials   Glass
Dimensions Various sizes
Manufacturer Burberry, UK
Website   www.burberry.com

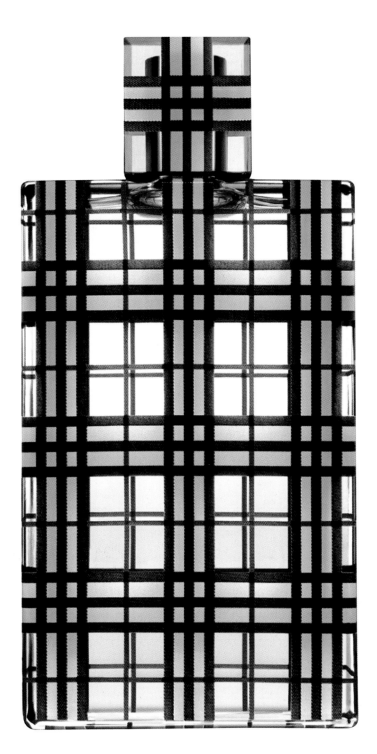

Product   Sideboards/storage units, Shanghai
Designer   Carlo Colombo
Materials   Aluminium
Dimensions   Various sizes
Manufacturer   Ycami, Italy
Website   www.ycami.com

Product	TV unit, table and bookcase with doors, Simplon
Designer	Jasper Morrison
Materials	Aluminium shelves or case, anodized aluminium legs
Dimensions	TV unit: L: 80 x H: 49 x W: 48cm (31 x 19 ¼ x 18 ⅞in)
	Table: L: 200 x H: 72 x W: 90cm (79 x 28 ⅜ x 35in)
	Bookcase with doors: L: 240 x H: 78 x W: 44 cm (94 x 31 x 17 ⅜in)
Manufacturer	Cap Design SpA, Italy
Website	www.cappellini.it

Product   Armchair, sofas, poufs, Oblong
Designer   Jasper Morrison
Materials   Polystyrene, fabric
Dimensions   Various sizes
Manufacturer Cap Design SpA, Italy
Website   www.cappellini.it

Product   Table, Tango
Designer   Stefano Giovannoni
Materials   Frame in bent steel plate, top in tempered glass
Dimensions   Various sizes
Manufacturer Magis SpA, Italy
Website   www.magisdesign.com

Product   Tap, Carmensita
Designer   Aldo Cibic
Materials   Chrome brass
Dimensions   H: 15 x D: 10cm (5 ⅞ x 3 ⅞in)
Manufacturer Rubinetteria Webert srl, Italy
Website   www.cibicpartners.com

Founder member of both Sottsass Associati and Memphis, Aldo Cibic may not enjoy the high profile of former co-partners Ettore Sottsass, Michele de Lucchi and Matteo Thun, yet his credentials are impeccable. Today, Cibic and Partners is one of the leading design studios in Italy. Active in the fields of architecture, interior design and industrial design, Cibic is probably best known for his public spaces – shops, restaurants, department stores, airports and hotels. Having moved away from the free forms and elite objects that we associate with Memphis, his product designs, while retaining post-modern creativity, have an eye for the commercial. Following Andrea Branzi's dictum, his aim is not only to 'design products for the home but to produce and sell them as well'. Blurring the boundaries between the artist and the industrialist, his designs combine clean functional lines with an emotional warmth and softness – he improves, softens and humanizes, taking inspiration from many sources and combining them into objects with universal appeal.

Product	Textile, Repeat Classic Stripe
Designer	Hella Jongerius
Materials	Cotton, rayon, polyester
Dimensions	W: 140cm (55in)
Manufacturer	Maharam, USA
Website	www.jongeriuslab.com
	www.maharam.com

Product   Height adjustable desk chair, Sheriff
Designer   Mats Theselius
Materials   Rivet prime leather, steel substructure
Dimensions H: 78–88 / (seat) 42–52 x W: 53 x D: 50cm
            (31–35 / 16 ½–20 ½ x 20 ⅞ x 19 ⅝in)
Manufacturer Källemo, Sweden
Website   www.kallemo.se

Product   Textile, Bespoke Stripe
Designer   Paul Smith
Materials   100% wool
Dimensions W: 140cm (55in)
Manufacturer Maharam, USA
Website   www.maharam.com

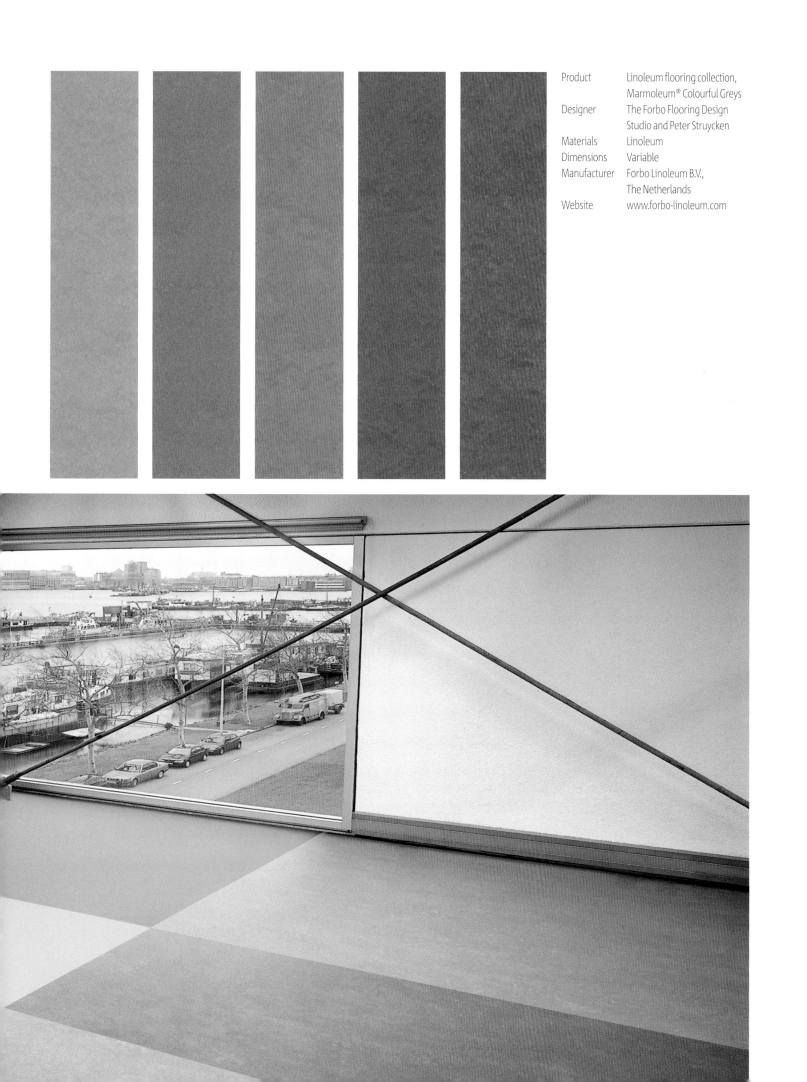

Product   Linoleum flooring collection,
               Marmoleum® Colourful Greys
Designer   The Forbo Flooring Design
               Studio and Peter Struycken
Materials   Linoleum
Dimensions   Variable
Manufacturer   Forbo Linoleum B.V.,
               The Netherlands
Website   www.forbo-linoleum.com

Product   Bookshelf, Hey chair
Designer   Maarten Baas
Materials   Vintages in a coating of epoxy
Dimensions   H: 175 x W: 80 x D: 50cm (69 x 31 x 19⅝in)
Manufacturer One-off, Maarten Baas, The Netherlands
Website   www.maartenbaas.com

'Hey Chair Be a Bookshelf' is bound to cause comment about the future of Dutch design. Is it sculpture, a set of shelves, or a commentary on perceived archetypes? Whatever, it's these kinds of objects that have resulted in articles such as Ron Kaal's polemic on Dutch design, published in *Frame* magazine's March/April 2004 edition. Considering Baas' charred chandelier, table and armchair, which he produced for Moooi in 2003, Kaal asks what these items have to do with design. 'The chair is not an original object, nor is it the result of a new technique or method of construction. It is simply the metamorphosis of an existing object, a product based on a gimmick, one of many gimmicks churned out by Dutch Design.' Kaal's piece is a critique not only of Baas' work, but also of the value of the conceptual, fresh and humorous products that we have come to associate with Dutch design in general and that have enjoyed unprecedented exposure over the past ten years. Not only Droog, which has erroneously been seen by many as synonymous with design from the Netherlands, but also the work of a range of individuals and companies that are redefining a Dutch national style.

What do we mean when we say something is typically Dutch? And why has the Netherlands engendered such a style? If we can set aside the output of the long-established Dutch commercial manufacturers – for example Spectrum, Artifort and Leolux – then what we are really talking about by Dutch design are individuals and small practices producing their work independently. These small batch productions are essentially but unorthodoxly plain, unpretentious, eclectic, illustrating an original use of materials, conceptually strong, often interdisciplinary, betraying a sense of humour and a concern for the environment. But how successful can this sort of design be in the international market place? Marcel Wanders sees that the essence of Dutch design has to be distilled into something more commercial for its influence to continue. Unsure whether one should, or indeed can, define national styles, he told me that what is generally considered to be Dutch design has had such a great impact on design worldwide because of 'its brutal, direct and sensitive way of speaking, because of the redefinition of imperfection and of material qualities as well as the notion that every industrial process is developed in a craft environment'. The anti-design nature of many of the products is a reaction to design being too impersonal and a way of endeavouring to create something more individual and warm. However, this should not be at the expense of making design too individual for the man in the street.

The Dutch have to move forward to survive. Design is taught at Eindhoven in a very academic way, students being tutored into creating a concept rather than coming up with a product that functions in any realistic way. Although Wanders believes that the Dutch approach has created a 'playing garden where beautiful and inspiring thoughts can grow', he finds it a terrible shame that so few products are designed for production and so do not end up in the lives of regular people. The mentality of the Dutch designer is still informed by the schoolroom and there is little connection with real industry or interest in producing an article that functions well. The Dutch 'style' both reflects and informs the current zeitgeist. What we expect from design is changing. There is a greater ideological freedom combined with new insights, technology and materials, which has given rise to unprecedented proposals in design. Objects are becoming illustrations of intentions, evoking experiences and establishing identities. There is a growing demand for a synergy between high-tech production methods and low-tech material – natural fibres, recyclable substances, simple and humane pieces – in other words stronger more ethical designs. Droog Design, and those that are following in their footsteps, have flourished in this environment and have in turn stimulated international discussion on design and brought experimentation and a pre-industrial arts-and-crafts design process back on the agenda. If this energy can be harnessed into something more commercial, then what we are seeing now could be only the tip of what The Netherlands has to offer.

Product	Conductor's baton, *Au Doigt et à la Baguette*
Designer	Paul Cocksedge
Materials	Rolled music paper
Dimensions	Approx. L: 30–33cm (11–13in)
Manufacturer	One-off, ECAL, Switzerland
Website	www.ecal.ch

A host of internationally acclaimed designers were asked by the Ecole Cantonale d'Art to reinterpret the conductor's baton. The result is an often amusing, sometimes thought-provoking and occasionally surreal collection of instruments that range from fetish to edible. During the Milan Furniture Fair 2004 the batons were displayed in the upstairs salon of the Gran Hotel de Milan, a room used by Verdi to write many of his masterpieces.

Product	Luxury aftermarket wheels for automobiles, Davin Revolution 5.1
Designer	David Fowlkes
Materials	Forged aluminium, spun aluminium
Dimensions	Diam: 24cm (10in)
Manufacturer	Limited production, Davin Wheel Company, USA
Website	www.davinwheels.com

Davin patented the technology for its spinning wheel for the LA Auto Show in 2001, but it was not until 2004, with the introduction of its new 'affordable luxury' range and fitments for more than 125 vehicles, that this dynamic effect hit the high street. A simple reinterpretation, the futuristically designed wheel consists of two elements – the base wheel and the spinner – which allow for continued revolution, even when the vehicle is stationary.

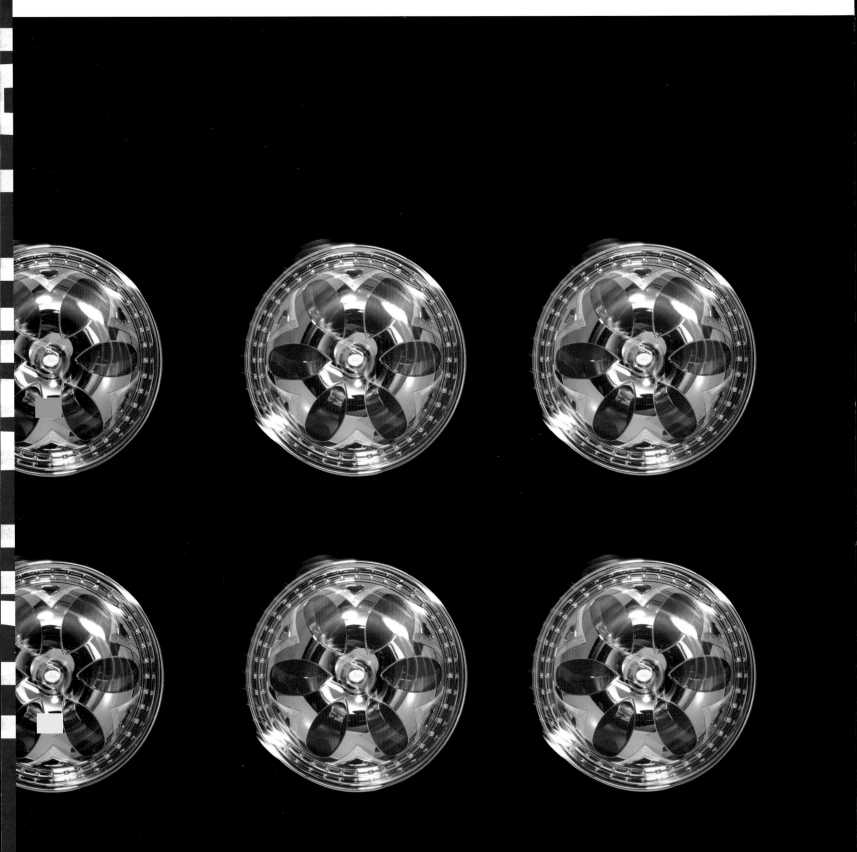

Product   Christmas tree, Silent Light
Designer   Tord Boontje, Alexander McQueen
Materials   Swarovski crystals, steel frame, rotation platform
               and mirror
Dimensions   H: 700 x W: 400 x D: 400cm (276 x 158 x 158in)
Manufacturer   One-off for the V&A Museum, London
Website   www.tordboontje.com

A blend of craft, naturalism and technology, Tord Boontje's work has become rather popular over the last couple of years, not least on the London design scene. His very affordable and successful 'Garland' lamp for Habitat can be found decorating many a light bulb across the land. He has collaborated with Alexander McQueen, creating a six-metre (20ft) high Christmas tree for the main hall of the Victoria and Albert Museum in 2003. Covered with 150,000 Swarovski crystals and mounted on a large turntable, the festive icon slowly revolved throughout the Christmas period to vibrant sparkling effect. The British Council brought Tord together with Paul Smith and Agent Provocateur. Along with Co-opa Roca, a women's handcrafts co-operative founded 20 years ago by Rio de Janeiro native Maria Teresa Leal, their designs were showcased in the Super Brands department of Selfridges as part of the London store's latest promotion, Brasil 40º. In addition, Boontje was asked to take part in the V&A's 'The Other Flower Show' during summer 2004, creating one of the 10 garden-shed installations by contemporary artists and designers. The V&A also selected him as one of the international designers who, from February to April 2004, was chosen to take part in the museum's first exhibition of contemporary lighting. The National Portrait Gallery, London, included a photograph of Tord in their 'Designer Faces' exhibition in 2003/4, *Blueprint* magazine nominated him as a finalist in their Product Designer of the Year, and in 2003 the Design Museum, London, selected him as their Designer of the Year.

Boontje's work is unashamedly decorative and appeals to the current zeitgeist away from the minimalism of the '90s and toward surface patterning and ornamentation. With garlands and drapery, glitter and sparkle, the ostentatious appearance of many of his designs could be considered frivolous, yet what separates them from the merely decorative is his research into new manufacturing processes and innovative materials. He combines motifs from nature with precision technology and industrial materials such as Tyvek and laser-cut, digitally printed fabrics, most recently combining these to create contemporary versions of the romantic aesthetics and richness of the seventeenth and eighteenth centuries in an unrestrained installation for Moroso at the Milan Furniture Fair 2004. Tord considers that his years at the Design Academy, Eindhoven, instilled in him the desire for experimentation, while his studies at the Royal College of Art in London gave him an awareness of the larger context in which design operates. He would readily admit that his design studio resembles more the classroom than an industrial practice, yet he is one of the few Dutch designers who have made the crossover between the purely conceptual and the commercially successful. By harnessing technology, he is able to create objects with high production values, new industrial processes enabling him to explore the sensual qualities he so admires, while producing mass-market lines in a non-labour-intensive way.

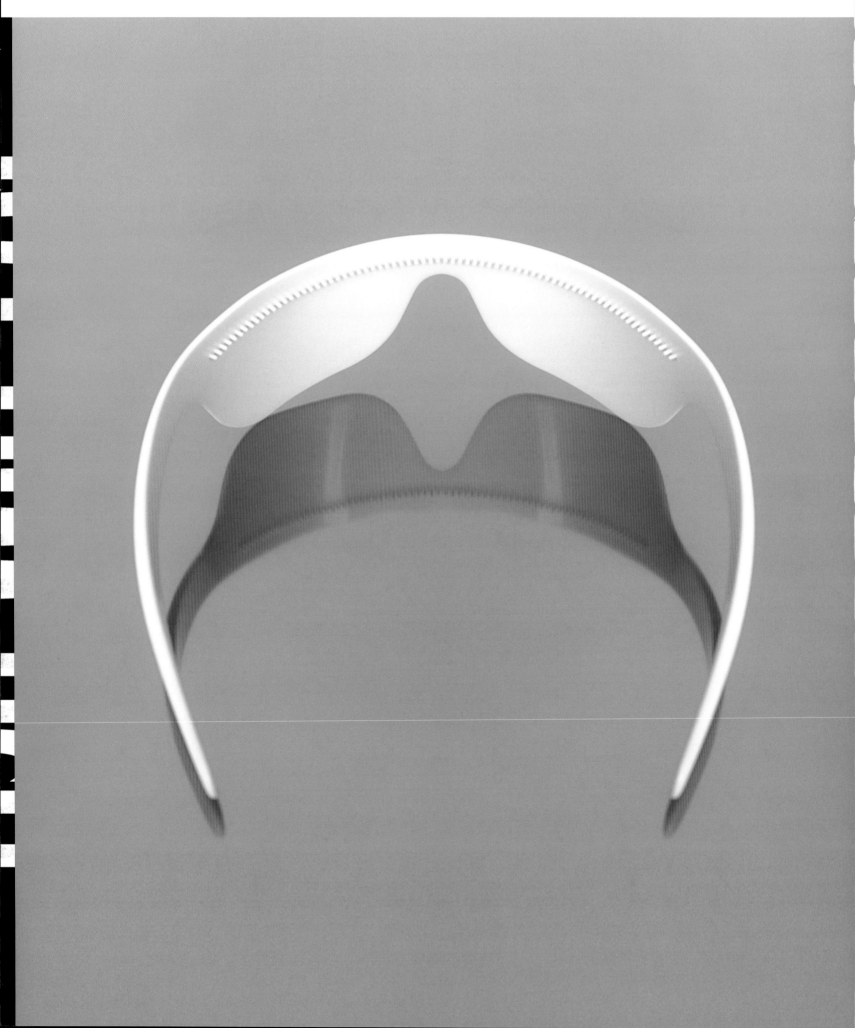

Product   Hairband, Hairglasses
Designer   Sam Hecht
Materials   ABS
Dimensions   H: 15 x W: 13 x D: 4cm (5 ⅞ x 5 ⅛ x 1 ⅝in)
Manufacturer iiii (Idea International), Japan
Website   www.industrialfacility.co.uk

Product   Chair/couch/bed, Hypnos
Designer   Alfredo Häberli
Materials   Chromium-plated steel, polyurethane with polyester
              filling, artificial leather, cover in fabric or leather
Dimensions   Various sizes
Manufacturer ClassiCon GmbH, Germany
Website   www.classicon.com

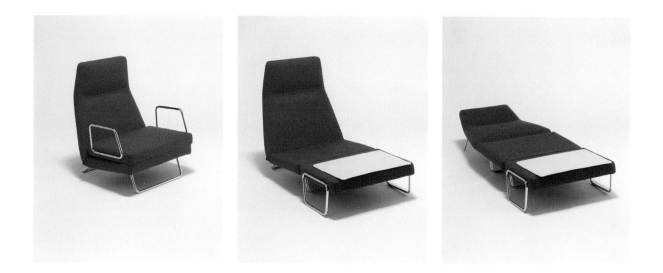

Product	Textiles, Repeat elements	Product	Fashion mobile phone with integrated camera and video,
Designer	Hella Jongerius		Nokia 7200
Materials	Cotton, rayon, polyester	Designer	Nokia Design Team
Dimensions	W: 140cm (55in)	Materials	Painted plastics and removable fabric/plastic covers
Manufacturer	Maharam, USA	Dimensions	H: 8.6 x W: 5 x D: 2.6cm (3 ⅜ x 2 x 1in)
Website	www.jongeriuslab.com	Manufacturer	Nokia, Finland
	www.maharam.com	Website	www.nokia.com

Product	Shelving unit, Hive H2
Designer	Chris Ferebee, 521 Design
Materials	Aluminium, wood veneer
Dimensions	(Single module) H: 33 x W: 140 x D: 32cm (13 x 55 x 12 ⅝in)
Manufacturer	Cinal Aps, Denmark
Website	www.fivetwentyonedesign.com

Product	Printed fabric, Saskia
Designer	Manuel Canovas
Materials	100% cotton
Dimensions	W: 143cm (56in)
Manufacturer	Manuel Canovas, Italy

Product	Washing machine, Dyson Two-Drums Allergy
Designer	Dyson Research and Development Team
Materials	Tub: high-strength polymer containing 40% glass; outer door made from the same material as riot shields
Dimensions	H: 84.8 x W: 59.5 x D: 57.5cm (33 x 23 ⅝ x 22 ⅞in)
Manufacturer	Dyson, UK
Website	www.dyson.com

According to Dyson's research, 15 minutes of hand washing produces cleaner clothes than 67 minutes in the best washing machine. By replacing the traditional one drum with two aligned drums that rotate in opposite directions, his patented design replicates manual action. The long wash and soak programmes are replaced by a shorter more rigorous process.

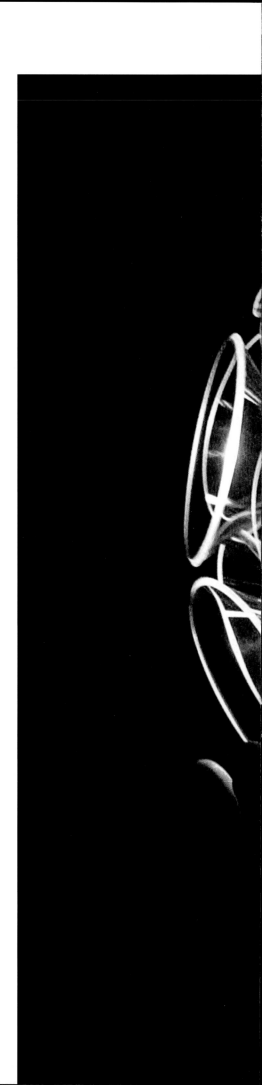

Product	Floor lamp, Dandelion
Designer	Deepdesign
Materials	Aluminium, PMMA, hi-power LEDs
Dimensions	H: 200 x Diam: 55cm (79 x 21 ⅝in)
Manufacturer	Tecno Delta, Italy
Website	www.deepdesign.it

Like its natural counterpart, Raffaella Mangiarotti's Dandelion Lamp is designed to catch any breeze and sways gently. However, unlike the flower, it's incapable of seeding itself.

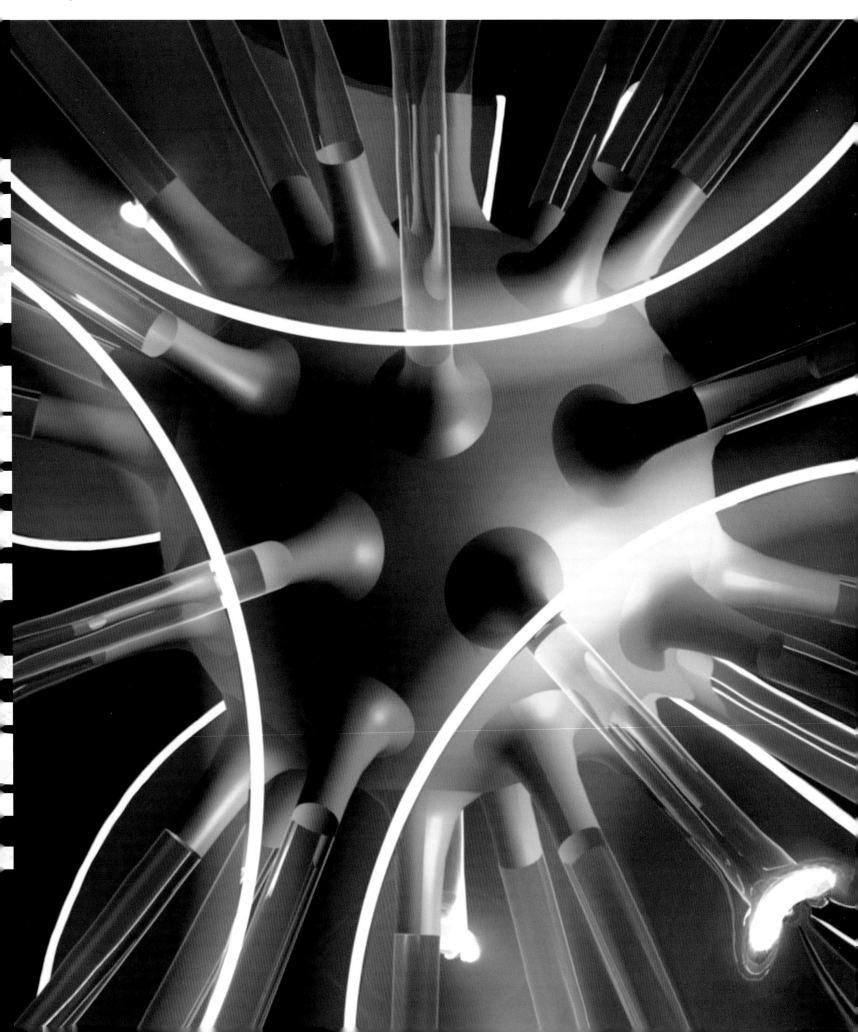

Product   Floor lamp, Dandelion
Designer   Deepdesign
Materials   Aluminium, PMMA, hi-power LEDs
Dimensions   H: 200 x Diam: 55cm (79 x 21 ⅝in)
Manufacturer Tecno Delta, Italy
Website   www.deepdesign.it

Product   Carpet, Kiki Carpet
Designer   Kiki van Eijk
Materials   100% wool
Dimensions   W: 300 x D: 200cm (118 x 79in)
Manufacturer Moooi, The Netherlands
Website   www.moooi.com

Product	Footwear, Adidas '1' running shoe
Designer	Scott Tomlinson, John Whiteman, Bob Lucas
Materials	Polyurethane, hytrel, polycarbonate, thermoplastic urethane, ethylene vinyl acetate
Dimensions	UK sizes 3 ½ – 13 ½
Manufacturer	Adidas, USA
Website	www.adidasus.com

After years of secrecy, Adidas has launched the first intelligent shoe, '1', with the claim that it will revolutionize the athletics industry. A sensor and a magnet monitor the cushioning level, a computer chip assessing whether it is too soft or too firm. By way of a motor-driven cable system, the shoe adapts to correct the amount of support needed throughout the whole run. In the last four years, Adidas has launched more product innovations than any other sports brand. The Roteiro seamless football; ClimaCool, a technology that helps athletes maintain optimum body temperature; and the Ground Control Suspension System for running and outdoor shoes, to name but a few.

Product   Blister for flowers, YG 1203 (Blister Collection)
Designer   Andrea Branzi
Materials   Moulded and sand-blasted plastic with magnetic closing,
             enamelled metal, blown glass
Dimensions   H: 47 x W: 49cm (18 ½ x 19¼in)
Manufacturer Limited batch production, Design Gallery Milano, Italy
Website   www.designgallerymilano.com

Product   Textiles, Repeat Dot Print
Designer   Hella Jongerius
Materials   Cotton, rayon, polyester
Dimensions   W: 140cm (55in)
Manufacturer Maharam, USA
Website   www.jongeriuslab.com www.maharam.com

Product   Multifunctional stroller, Bugaboo Frog
Designer   Max Barenbrug
Materials   Aluminium, nylon with glass fibre
Dimensions   (Unfolded) H: 106 x W: 60 x L: 95cm (42 x 23 ⅝ x 37in)
               (Folded) H: 23 x W: 50 x L: 89 (9 x 19 ⅝ x 35in)
Manufacturer   Bugaboo, The Netherlands
Website   www.bugaboo.nl

Product	Wallpaper, Wallpaper Made by Rats
Designer	Front
Materials	Paper
Dimensions	W: 50 x L: 1000cm (19 ⅝ x 394in)
Manufacturer	Front, Sweden
Website	www.frontdesign.se

Four young women – Sofia Lagerkvist, Katja Sävström, Anna Lindgren and Charlotte von der Lancken – forming the Swedish design group Front came up with an intriguing exhibition for the Salon Satellite show at the Milan Furniture Fair 2004. Part of the design of each of a series of objects was determined by an external factor or event that affected the design process at random. A hole created by a controlled explosion was turned into a cast for a soft chair, plastic heated and draped like a textile became a curtain-like screen, a UV-sensitive wallpaper changes pattern with the sunlight, and a vase was made with a built-in fall – its shape is repeated and stuck together throughout the path of its descent from shelf to floor.

A large part of the show, however, was given over to objects that had been influenced by the activities of animals. 'We asked animals to help us out. "Sure we'll help you out", they answered. "Make something nice", we told them. And so they did.' Ceramic vases were cast from dog tracks in the deep snow and a lampshade was produced based on a fly's path around a light bulb, which was recorded by motion-capture camera. The rat wallpaper, illustrated here, was created by allowing rodents – I don't like to say rats as this is obviously a gerbil – to gnaw on rolls of pre-manufactured wallpaper, the holes created making a repetitive pattern that reveals the old wall covering to which the new wallpaper is glued.

In this controlled world, it's a relief to see design that is out of control.
Wieki Somers

Product   Wallpaper, Wallpaper Made by Rats
Designer   Front
Materials   Paper
Dimensions   W: 50 x L: 1000cm (19 ⅝ x 394in)
Manufacturer Front, Sweden
Website   www.frontdesign.se

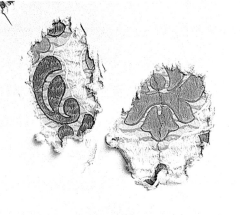

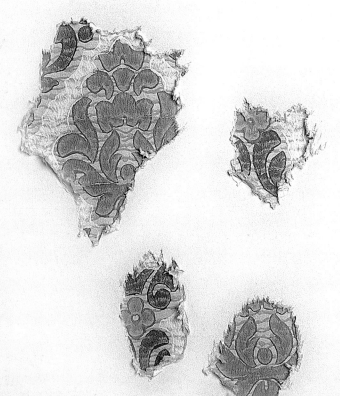

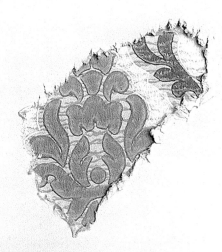

Product	Lighting, Flames
Designer	Chris Kabel
Materials	Metal construction with standard gas cylinder
Dimensions	H: 55 x W: 22 x D: 10cm (21 ⅝ x 8 ⅝ x 3 ⅞in)
Manufacturer	Moooi, The Netherlands
Website	www.moooi.com

I've tried it, and the inventor of the candle would turn in his grave. It's a really ingenious thing and gives a much more exiting light than a candle.
Joris Laarman

Product	Bookshelf, Anna Morph
Designer	Matthew Sindall
Materials	Printed melamine, stainless steel
Dimensions	H: 155 x W: 115 x D: 38cm (61 x 45 x 15in)
Manufacturer	Sawaya & Moroni SpA, Italy
Website	www.sawayamoroni.com

Whether it's a 'devil may care' reaction to the depressing state of the world today or a desire to get away from the past years of clean and severe minimalist designs, an emphasis on surface patterning is a trend that has presented itself throughout 2004–5. In particular, a veritable bouquet of colourful floral motifs has found its way onto objects and accessories.

Matthew Sindall, born in the UK but presently working in France, is not noted for flourishes of light-heartedness in his work. Chief designer in the architectural practices of MET Studios in London and then with Jean-Michel Wilmotte in Paris, his portfolio since going solo in 1995 consists more of heavy-duty industrial design – street lighting for Ecaltec, UV

transmission consoles for Guinot, seating for SNCF and publicity panels for Banque du Luxembourg. Yet for several years now he has been successfully collaborating with Sawaya & Moroni on a growing line of furniture.

Most recently, Sindall has photographed flowers and geometric subjects and printed the image onto transparent melamine, which he has wrapped around wooden structures to form 'Anna Morph', a limited-edition collection of bookshelves. Although at first glance these shelves may look like any other decorated piece, they are cleverly based on the sixteenth-century artifice 'annamorphose', where an image was painted in a distorted way only to be understood when a mirrored cone or cylinder was placed in the centre of the painting. Similarly, the image on the 'Anna Morph' bookcase is broken down and becomes comprehensible from only three viewpoints (right, frontal and left).

Sindall told me that his work concentrates on perception, whether tactile, visual or latent: 'I try to imbue other values into a piece of furniture, offering the user different levels of interaction by working with materials and techniques.' He sees print as a modern type of marquetry and, with the advances made in printing processes, believes that personalized furniture will become more accessible, with owners able to select the images they want to decorate their surfaces.

Product	Ceramic tile with integrated LED lighting,
	Mosa Terra Maestricht
Designer	Royal Mosa Design Team
Materials	Unglazed ceramic tiles
Dimensions	Various sizes
Manufacturer	Royal Mosa, The Netherlands
Website	www.mosa.nl

Advanced lighting technology allows LEDs to be placed in ceramic tiles to striking effect. Of the same size, thickness and quality, they sit seamlessly alongside other tiles, the light passing through a tiny square or circular aperture in the centre.

Product	Tableware, coffee pot and cups (Black Gold Collection)
Designer	Ineke Hans
Materials	Black porcelain
Dimensions	Coffee pot: Diam: 18.5 x H: 22 (7 ¼ x 8 ⅝in)
	Cup: Diam: 13.5 x H: 5cm (5 ⅜ x 2in)
Manufacturer	Limited batch production, Ineke Hans/Arnhem,
	The Netherlands
Website	www.inekehans.com

Product	Table, Plaintable
Designer	Stephanie Ziegler and Ulrich Goss, gossindustrialdesign
Materials	Table legs: bent aluminium profile; under construction: glassfibre-reinforced plastics; table top: 4mm alucobond with 0.6 mm bamboo veneer; variable inlay module: ceramic or heat-resistant plastic
Dimensions	H: 74 x W: 100 x L: 250cm (29 ⅛ x 39 x 98in)
Manufacturer	Prototype, gossindustrialdesign
Website	www.gossindustrialdesign.de

Product	Children's chair, Seggiolina Pop
Designer	Enzo Mari
Materials	Expanded polypropylene
Dimensions	H: 55 (seat: 30cm) x W: 28 x D: 32.5cm
	(21 ⅝/11 ¾ x 11 x 13in)
Manufacturer	Magis SpA, Italy
Website	www.magisdesign.com

Product	Chair, Mars
Designer	Konstantin Grcic
Materials	Synthetic resin, removable cover in fabric
	or leather
Dimensions	H: 75/(seat) 44 x W: 47 x D: 54cm
	(29 ½ /17 ⅜ x 18 ½ x 21 ¼in)
Manufacturer	ClassiCon GmbH, Germany
Website	www.classicon.com

Product	Compass watch, Altimer (Oregon series)
Designer	Scott Wilson and Jason Martin
Materials	Solid forged aluminium or titanium, polyurethane, mineral glass
Dimensions	Diam: 5 x D: 1.6cm (2 x ⅝in)
Manufacturer	Nike Inc., USA
Website	www.nike.com

Product	Mobile living unit, Loftcube
Designer	Werner Aisslinger
Materials	Steel, wood, ABS
Dimensions	H: 680 x W: 410 x D: 410cm (268 x 162 x 162in)
Manufacturer	Limited edition, Studio Aisslinger
Website	www.aisslinger.de

Werner Aisslinger's 'Loftcube' adds a new dimension to the concept of escaping the hurly-burly of city life. Adding thousands to the property value of any urban flat, roof gardens have always been desired and sought after by a generation of city-dwellers who seek privacy, tranquillity and escape from the hectic and stressful world below. Add to this a self-contained living unit and the possibilities are endless – a whole new community living on the roof tops. With Bauhaus aesthetic and largely glazed walls, the unit offers

an open-plan living, cooking and dining area with a separate sleeping space and a bathroom. Optional extras include customized furniture and even a swimming pool. According to Aisslinger's studio, people with flat roofs aren't the only ones that are showing interest in the cube. They have had orders from houseboats, from home-owners with large gardens and consumers who simply want a holiday home. Aisslinger's idea is not a new one. The space-age craze of the 1960s inspired new ways of looking at the way we live, utopian architecture that encapsulated the ideas of mobility, increased leisure time and new material. Matti Suuronen's 'Futuro' house must have been in Aisslinger's mind when he designed the 'Loftcube'. Like the 'Futuro' house, it is lightweight and can be easily transported to any desired location by helicopter.

Werner Aisslinger's loftcube is a true ode to freedom, an urban tree house. Too bad about the interior, but I would love to build this one myself sometime.
Joris Laarman

Product	Rug/Nightlight, Baby Zoo/Good Night
Designer	Laurene Leon Boym
Materials	Injection-moulded polycarbonate; laminated cellulose with a chrome aluminium sheet; injection-moulded, self-extinguishing PA6 polyamide; pure virgin wool; LED
Dimensions	(Carpet) W: 150 x L: 150cm (59 x 59in)
	(Lamp) H: 3.3cm x Diam: 18cm (1 ⅜ x 7 ⅛in)
Manufacturer	Flos SpA, Italy
Website	www.boym.com

The 'Baby Zoo' range of rugs is designed to interact with the Flos 'Good Night' light. The comforting colour-changing lamp sits on the spot indicated, changing night to day.

Product   Storage system, Layout
Designer   Michele De Lucchi
Materials   Extruded aluminium, MDF
Dimensions   Various sizes
Manufacturer   Alias SpA, Italy
Website   www.aliasdesign.it

Product   Storage system, Layout
Designer   Michele De Lucchi
Materials   Extruded aluminium, MDF
Dimensions   Various sizes
Manufacturer   Alias SpA, Italy
Website   www.aliasdesign.it

Product   Hand-held electronic kitchen tools, 101.013
Designer   Chris Christou, Youmeus Design Ltd
Materials   ABS, polypropylene, rubber, steel
Dimensions   H: 32 x Diam: 7cm (12 ⅝ x 2 ¾in)
Manufacturer Kenwood Ltd, UK
Website   www.youmeusdesign.com

Product	Modular table system, Joyn
Designer	Ronan and Erwan Bouroullec
Materials	Powder-coated MDF, melamine-faced particleboard, powder-coated aluminium, powder-coated sheet shell, fabrics, leather, polyurethane, polypropylene
Dimensions	H: 72 x W: 180 x L: 440cm (28 ⅜ x 71 x 173in)
Manufacturer	Vitra, Switzerland
Website	www.vitra.com

Product	Seating system, Plastics
Designer	Piero Lissoni
Materials	Pouf and armchair: fabric-covered soft polyurethane,
	transparent polycarbonate
	Small table: transparent polycarbonate
Dimensions	Pouf: H: 32 x W: 90 x D: 90cm (12 ⅝ x 35 x 35in)
	Armchair: H: 60 x W: 90 x D: 90cm (23 ⅝ x 35 x 35in)
	Small table: H: 12 x W: 90 x L: 110 x cm (4 ¾ x 35 x 43in)
Manufacturer	Kartell SpA, Italy
Website	www.kartell.it

Product   Collection of drinking glasses, Shorties
Designer   James Irvine
Materials   Glass
Dimensions   Various sizes
Manufacturer   Covo srl, Italy
Website   www.covo.it

Product   Armchair, Ombra
Designer   Charlotte Perriand
Materials   Steel, upholstered in fabric or leather
Dimensions   H: 65 x L: 70 x D: 82cm (25 ⅝ x 27 ½ x 32in)
Manufacturer Cassina SpA, Italy
Website   www.cassina.it

The Milan Furniture Fair is generally regarded as the barometer by which to measure the health, or not, of the contemporary furniture industry during the preceding 12 months. Although the 2004 show was bigger than ever, with 188,000 visitors seeking out the *crème de la crème* among the 19,000 exhibitors, it was disheartening to see even the biggest manufacturing companies playing it safe with conservative lines, neutral colours, extensions of existing ranges and re-editions. Cassina was a case in point. Although they presented Starck's M.I.S.S. audio-visual sofa (see pages 130–1), the rest of their exhibition was devoted to re-editions by the Modernist designer Charlotte Perriand. Not that one can fault this line of furniture – and it forms an addition to their 'I Maestri' series, which since the mid '60s has re-edited design classics by Le Corbusier, Gerrit Thomas

Rietveld, Charles Rennie Mackintosh, Erik Gunnar Asplund and Frank Lloyd Wright. In the case of Cassina, indeed, it could be argued that choosing to highlight the work of Perriand has less to do with a conservative attitude being the safest approach to the present unsettled economic climate and more a genuine conviction that works by masters of the Modern Movement can become fertile soil for designers today.

Perriand's work has a contemporary feel. In 1937, after having spent ten years in Le Corbusier's studio, where she was in charge of the furniture and fittings programme, she was invited by the Ministry of Trade and Industry of Japan to advise on industrial design. Once in Japan, Perriand was influenced by the tradition of Japanese furniture making, which appeared close to her own taste for the standardization of elements,

harmony of forms and volumes, architectural flexibility and the care given to the environment. It's the East meets West style of the designs that followed that lends Perriand's work such an immediate appeal to young designers today.

The 'Ombra' easy chair, which she originally designed in Tokyo in 1953 for her husband's house, combines a minimalist language and structure with maximum functionality and is the result of what Perriand described as 'a synthesis of the arts' of European and Japanese cultures. This contemporary version has changed steel structure and square cushions for seating and backrests, interlinked by a zipper, rather than a single sheet of curved ply board, yet the result retains the qualities of density and lightness of the reference piece.

1

2

3

4

5

6

A Flavour of 2003/4

(1) Fondation Cartier presents Kelvin 40, a concept jet designed by Marc Newson.

(2) Exhibition of Baas' customized furniture classics at Murray Moss' store, New York.

(3) Habitat invites 22 celebrities from the worlds of film, literature, fashion and sports to design products for its stores to celebrate its 40th anniversary. Personalities involved with the V.I.P. (Very Important Product) range include the actor Ewan McGregor, retired formula one racing driver Stirling Moss, super-model Helena Christensen (her decorative light is shown), boxer Lennox Lewis and author Louis de Bernières.

(4) The Bouroullec and Campana brothers design ideal houses for IMM Cologne; Hella Jongerius and Patricia Urquiola are invited to supply their ideas for 2005.

(5) The Bombay Sapphire Blue Room glass design award is presented to Paul Cocksedge.

(6) Marks and Spencer poach Vittorio Radice from Selfridges for £1.2 million, but the high-profile

general merchandise director leaves within a year of taking up his appointment.

Cedric Price, the British architect, promoter of life-long learning and brownfield regeneration, dies at the age of 68.

Sir Terence Conran is appointed Provost of the Royal College of Art, London.

The production of Boeing's new all-composite B7E7 'Dreamliner' plane contributes to a world shortage of aerospace-quality carbon fibre. Supplies of 'commercial'-grade fibres are also critically low.

The Cooper Hewitt National Design Awards are presented to I.M. Pei and Lella and Massimo Vignelli (Lifetime Achievement) and to Herman Miller (Product Design).

Centraal Museum, Utrecht, buys the rare 'Lattenleun' chair designed in 1918 by Gerrit Thomas Rietveld for €115.000.

Dutch office furniture giant Ahrend buys Gispen.

Philippe Starck and Romain Hatchuel launch a strategic and integrated communications consultancy, 'The Key', to act as a bridge between Asian manufacturers and global markets.

Poltrona Frau sells 30 per cent of its shares to 'Charme', an investment fund managed by the Italian industrialist and Ferrari Chairman Luca Cordero di Montezemolo. With the proceeds it is able to acquire Cappellini, Thonet Vienna and Gufram.

Architecture critic Paul Goldberger becomes Dean of the Parson's School of Design, New York.

British Design Museum selects the UK product designer Daniel Brown as its Designer of the Year.

The family-run Italian manufacturing company B&B Italia sells 55 per cent of its shares to 'Opera', an investment fund backed by jewellery group Bulgari.

The Conran Foundation Collection at the British Design Museum is selected by Thomas Heatherwick.

7

8

9

10

11

12

(7) Museum Boijmans Van Beuningen in Rotterdam purchases an original 'Mae West Lips' sofa designed in 1936 by Salvador Dali from Christie's, London, for €75,000. Bd Ediciones de Diseno reissues this famous work in collaboration with Oscar Tusquets to commemorate the centenary of Dali's birth.

(8) Marks and Spencer's Lifestore opens in Tyne and Wear in the north of England. The megastore contains a full-sized two-storey house designed by John Pawson. Pawson also acts as consultant on the project and is responsible for the interior of the shop and aspects of the exterior. The graphics and store identity are designed by former *Wallpaper* editor Tyler Brûlé.

(9) Karim Rashid becomes a DJ.

(10) Marc Newson and Richard Allen design the Australian team's outfits for the opening ceremony of the Olympic games .

(11) Microsoft officially unveils a new optical mouse designed by Philippe Starck.

(12) The Jerwood Applied Arts Prize 2003 is dedicated to glass design and awarded to Helen Maurer.

The Manager and owner of IKEA, Ingvar Kamprad, surpasses Bill Gates of Microsoft as the richest man on earth. His wealth is estimated at $53 billion. IKEA denies the report, stating that Kamprad donated the concern to the Dutch Stichting Ingka Foundation in 1982.

The Design Academy, Eindhoven is called 'best in world' by *The New York Times.*

Droog Design celebrates its 10+1 Anniversary with a series of European exhibitions.

The Blueprint Design Award is presented to Jonathan Ives.

The special 50th anniversary Compasso d'Oro prize is awarded to Giulio Castelli, founder of Kartell, president of the ADI foundation and president of Fondazione Cosmit.

Zaha Hadid is awarded the Pritkzer Prize.

In a return to its roots, German furniture company Vitra produces a new line of domestic furnishings, 'Vitra at Home'. The debut collection includes new designs by Jasper Morrison and Ronan and Erwan Bouroullec, as well as revived classics by Charles and Ray Eames, George Nelson and Verner Panton, among others.

Hella Jongerius is cited Designer of the Year at the Salon du Meuble, Paris.

The Groninger Museum in The Netherlands holds the first major European retrospective of Marc Newson's work.

Tragedy hits IKEA at the launch of its latest store in Jeddah, Saudi Arabia. Massive crowds combined with high temperature and humidity levels leave two dead and many suffering from heat exhaustion and fatigue.

Marcel Wanders becomes Guest Editor of *The International Design Yearbook 2005.*

Patricia Urquiola and Tord Boontje dominate the design press.

Biographies

Eero Aarnio was born in 1932 in Helsinki, Finland, where he studied at the Institute of Industrial Arts. He began working with plastics in 1960, opening his own studio in 1962. Aarnio created two of the most famous chairs of the 1960s, the 'Globe' and the 'Gyro'. 60–1

Werner Aisslinger was born in Berlin in 1964. He founded his own company in 1993 and since then has undertaken furniture and corporate architecture projects for companies such as Cappellini, Magis and Lufthansa. 42, 218–9

Apple's Industrial Design team, led by Jonathan Ive, grabbed the world's attention in 1998 with the release of the first iMac. More than two million iMacs were sold in the first year and *BusinessWeek* cited its design as 'one of the century's lasting images'. The iMac went on to win many design competitions, including Best of Category in *ID* magazine, a Gold Award from the UK-based educational charity D&AD and Object of the Year by *The Face* magazine. The team is responsible for the design of all Apple's products, including the ground-breaking new iMac, Power Mac G5, PowerBook G4 and the phenomenally popular iPod and iPod mini. 109

Ron Arad was born in Tel Aviv, Israel in 1951 and studied at the Jerusalem Academy of Art and at the Architectural Association in London. In 1981 he co-founded One Off. In 1988 he won the Tel Aviv Opera Foyer Interior Competition and formed Ron Arad Associates the following year in order to realize the project. Other projects include furniture design for Poltronova, Vitra, Moroso, Alessi, The Gallery Mourmans and Driade and the interiors of the Belgo restaurants in London. In 2000 he had a major retrospective at the Victoria & Albert Museum, London. His work is included in several public collections worldwide and has been featured in numerous exhibitions and publications. Arad is currently professor of furniture design at the Royal Academy of Art in London. 23, 58, 72–3

Archirivolto is a design and architecture studio in Siena, Italy. It was established in 1983 by Claudio Dondoli and Marco Pocci, who met while studying architecture in Florence. 128

Antoni Arola is an interior and industrial designer born in Tarragona, Spain in 1960. He started his professional career in 1984 at the Liévore & Pensi Studio in Barcelona and in 1990 enrolled in the Associate Designers company before opening his own studio in Barcelona in 1994. He is known for his lighting designs for Santa & Cole and Metalarte, sofa collections for Temas V, perfume bottles for Armand Basi, Angel Schlesser and Loewe and bathroom furnishings for ArtQuitect. Interior design projects include the Oven and Mos restaurants and the Cacao Sampaka shop, the latter awarded with the FAD prize. He has won two silver Delta Industrial Design awards and Spain's 2003 National Design Prize. 142

Dodo Arslan studied industrial design at the Istituto Europeo di Design in Milan, Italy (1994–8). After three years in design consultancies, he opened his own studio in Milan. He now works as a consultant for Design Continuum, the Istituto Europeo di Design's Research Centre and teaches there and at Scuola Italiana Design in Padova. In 2003 he began to develop furniture products. 86–7

Enrico Azzimonti was born in Italy in 1966 and studied architecture and design in Milan. He runs his own design studio in Busto Arsizio, Italy. 135

Azumi Shin and Tomoko Azumi were born in Japan in 1950 and 1952 respectively. Both studied industrial design at Kyoto City University of Art and the Royal College of Art, London. They founded Azumi's in 1995. 123, 143

Maarten Baas was born in Arnsberg, The Netherlands in 1978 and studied at the Design Academy Eindhoven. His clients include Pol, s Potten and Moooi. His designs have been exhibited and published many times. 188–9

Ralph Ball is a furniture and lighting designer and professor of design at Central Saint Martins College of Art and Design in London. He has won several design awards in the UK and USA, has exhibited widely in Europe, Japan and the USA and his work is in permanent collections in the UK and USA. In 2000 he launched Studio Ball Art and Design with Maxine Naylor and his brother, artist Keith Ball. 21

Barber Osgerby was formed in 1996 by Edward Barber and Jay Osgerby, who met while studying at the Royal College of Art in London. Since then, they have been developing design collections for leading manufacturers and clients and their designs have been exhibited worldwide and won numerous design awards. Their 'Loop Table' is in the permanent collections of the Victoria & Albert Museum, London and the Metropolitan Museum of Art, New York and their 'Shell Table' has been nominated for the Compasso d'Oro 2004. In 2001 Edward Barber and Jay Osgerby formed Universal Design Studio, a multi-disciplinary company, specializing in architectural, industrial design and interior projects. 62–3, 148–9

Max Barenbrug, an industrial designer, formed Bugaboo in 1999 with Eduard Zanen, a medical doctor and sales director. Max designed the first 'Bugaboo Frog' for his final project at the Design Academy Eindhoven in 1994. He graduated with honours and was awarded Best Design of the Year. Bugaboo, which has its headquarters in Amsterdam, is a fast-growing company: it has already opened offices in Spain, the UK and the USA, and the 'Bugaboo Frog', which has undergone many changes since the 1994 graduation project, is sold in 21 countries. 206

Fabien Baron was born in Pars in 1959 but moved to New York in 1982 where he became art director of Italian *Vogue* and *Interview*. In 1992, he was appointed creative director of *Harper's Bazaar*. A legend in the worlds of fashion, magazine design and advertising, he also designs furniture. 178

Bartoli Design is the corporate name of six design professionals who have been working together since 1999: Albertina Amadeo, Anna Bartoli, Carlo Bartoli, Paolo Bartoli, Paolo Crescenti and Giulio Ripamonti. Bartoli's clients include Arclinea, Arflex, Colombo Design, Confalonieri, Delight, Deltacalor, Kartell, Kristalia, Laurameroni Design Collection, Matteograssi, Multipla 2000, Rossi di Albizzate, Sagsa, Segis, Steelcase Strafor, Tisettanta, Varenna-Poliform and Ycami. 79

Yves Béhar is a graduate of the Art Center College of Design in Pasadena, California and was design leader at frogdesign and Lunar design before founding the San Francisco-based design studio Fuseproject. Béhar's design strategy involves focusing on the emotional experience of the user and communicating it through storytelling. In 2004 the San Francisco Museum of Modern Art exhibited a solo show of Béhar's diverse work, a 'futurespective' that spanned products, fashion, graphics, packaging, environments and strategy. Fuseproject's recent clients include Herman Miller, Birkenstock, Swarovski, MINI, Hussein Chalayan, Toshiba, Nike and Hewlett-Packard. 137, 140, 167

Tord Boontje was born in 1968 in Enschede, The Netherlands. He studied industrial design at the Design Academy Eindhoven before moving to the UK to study at the Royal College of Art in London. He uses industrial technologies to create exquisite glassware, lighting and furniture. 76–7, 111, 191

Ronan and Erwan Bouroullec are brothers who have collaborated since 1998. Erwan studied industrial design in Paris at the Ecole Nationale Supérieure des Arts Appliqués and the Ecole Nationale Supérieure des Arts Decoratifs. Ronan graduated in applied and decorative art and has worked freelance since 1995, designing objects and furniture for Liaigre, Cappellini, Ligne Roset and Galerie Neotu. He was awarded Best Designer at the ICFF, New York in 1999. 138–9, 224–5

Laurene Leon Boym was born in New York City, where she studied at the School of Visual Arts and the Pratt Institute. Since 1994, she has been a partner in Boym Partners Inc, bringing humour and fun to products and exhibitions. Boym was a founder of the Association of Women Industrial Designers (AWID) in 1992, co-curating 'Goddess In the Details' in 1995 and running the organization between 1995 and 1997. She has been a teacher of product design at Parsons School of Design, New York since 1995. 220

Andrea Branzi is an architect, designer and critic, who was born in Florence but now lives and works in Milan. He was a member of Archizoom Associati, the Italian avant-garde group of radical design, until 1974 and in 1983 was among the founders of the Domus Academy, a postgraduate school of design. In 1987 he was awarded the Special Compasso d'Oro for his work as a designer and theorist. He has held many exhibitions of his work, including at the Musée des Arts Décoratifs in Paris and at the Museum of Modern Art in New York. He has written several books on design and has held lectures all over the world. 169, 204

Debbie Jane Buchan was born in Edinburgh, Scotland in 1973. She studied textiles at the Gray's School of Art at the Robert Gordon University in Aberdeen, graduating with an MA in surface communication in 1996. In her work she is concerned with 'smart' fabrics and pushing the boundaries between design disciplines through the innovative use of applications and technologies. 52–3, 67, 99, 102–3, 112–13, 137, 145, 146–7, 152–3

Sam Buxton was born in London in 1972. He studied furniture design at Middlesex University before enrolling at the Royal College of Art in 1997. After graduation he set up two design studios with fellow RCA graduates. Now working on his own, Buxton has developed projects for Kenzo, Bloomberg and Vauxhall as well as the burgeoning MIKRO-Man collection, which is now expanding into environments with a stainless-steel fold up MIKRO-House. His work has been exhibited widely from Brazil to Australia, Japan and Italy. He was one of the four designers short-listed for the Design Museum's Designer of the Year award in 2004. 95

Ferdinando and Humberto Campana have been working together, based in São Paolo, Brazil, since 1983. The brothers, who produce political rather than merely functional objects, were thrust into the limelight with their 1989 exhibition 'The Inconsolable'. Their radical vision involves using traditional materials and industrial surplus to create an independent Brazilian design language. 82–3

Chris Christou graduated with first class honours from Ravensbourne College of Design & Communication in Greater London and joined kdo in 1994 at its inception, where his work involved strategic design programmes for international brands such as Kenwood & Ariete. In 2000 Chris

Christou established his own practice, Future Creative, where his projects included product, packaging and interior design and art direction. He has implemented comprehensive design strategies for clients in the fields of transportation, technology, food preparation and tableware. In 2003 he co-founded Youmeus Design Ltd, a new generation design and innovation company focused on communicating the brand equity of corporations through products. Christou has won several design awards and has chaired a number of award juries for Design & Art Direction (D&AD) and The Audi Design Foundation. His work has also been featured in numerous publications worldwide and museum collections such as Die Neue Sammlung in Munich. 122, 223

Aldo Cibic was born in Schio, Italy in 1955. He moved to Milan in 1979 to work with Ettore Sottsass, becoming his partner the following year, together with Matteo Thun and Marco Zanini. That same year marked the creation of Memphis, of which Cibic was one of the designers and founders. He founded Cibic & Partners with Antonella Spiezio in 1989, working on his own projects and for other companies, as well as expanding into the field of interior design and architecture projects in Italy and abroad. 183

Kenneth Cobonpue studied industrial design at the Pratt Institute in New York and furniture marketing and production at the Export Akademie Baden-Württemberg in Reutlingen, Germany. He worked in Bielefeld and Munich before returning home to Cebu, Philippines in 1996 to manage Interior Crafts of the Islands, Inc., a furniture design and manufacturing company founded in 1972 by his mother Betty. Cobonpue's work has earned him international recognition. 119, 121

Paul Cocksedge was born in London in 1978 and studied industrial design at Sheffield Hallam University and product design at the Royal College of Art in London. In 2003 he opened a studio with Joana Pinho, who he met at the RCA. The same year he won the Bombay Sapphire Glass prize. In 2004 Cocksedge was short-listed for the London Design Museum's Designer of the year prize. His designs have been exhibited worldwide. 191

Carlo Colombo was born in Carimate in 1967 and graduated in architecture with a specialization in industrial design from the Polytechnic Institute of Milan. His professional career began with Studio Pusinelli in Como, where he worked on projects in Africa and Russia. From 1990–2 he worked in photography and designed objects, which resulted in his later collaboration with Cappellini. Other clients include Ycami and Flexiform. 179

Nick Crosbie is the design director of Inflate Design Ltd in London. 32–3

Lorenzo Damiani was born in Lissone (Mi) in 1972. His designs have been awarded several times. Clients include Campeggi, Cappellini and Montina. 164

Michele De Lucchi was born in Italy in 1951. He has won international renown as an architect and was a leading force in the Cavart Group during the Radical Design years and a founder member of the Memphis group. Clients include Arflex, Artemide, Kartell, Deutsche Bank, Olivetti, Alias. 221, 222

Deepdesign was formed in 1998 in Milan by Matteo Bazzicalupo and Raffaella Mangiarotti. Deepdesign has been exploring innovative design of electronic products, white goods, furniture and food. Clients include Barilla, Castelli Haworth, CocaCola, Giorgetti, Kraft, Imetec, Mandarina Duck and San Lorenzo. 198–9

Tom Dixon was born in Sfax, Tunisia in 1959 but moved to the UK when he was four years old. A self-taught designer, he is now the Creative Director of Habitat UK and also runs his own design studio. 158–9

The Dyson Research and Development Team is committed to researching and developing new products and technology that work better. The team, which is based in Malmesbury, Wiltshire, UK, numbers 1,200 people, including 350 engineers and scientists, who design, develop and engineer all new Dyson products and technology, as well as challenge and develop existing technologies. Dyson has 850 patents and patent applications for more than 120 inventions. 198

Daniel Eltner was born in 1970 and studied industrial design in Munich. He has been working freelance as a designer for WMF AG, Geislingen since 1997. 160–1

El Ultimo Grito was founded in 1997 by Roberto Feo and Rosario Hurtado. Roberto Feo was born in London in 1964 but grew up in Madrid, Spain. He studied furniture design at the London College of Furniture and completed an MA in Furniture Design at the Royal College of Art. Rosario Hurtado was born in Madrid in 1966 and moved to London in 1989 to study cabinet making and furniture design at the London College of Furniture. She completed her BA in industrial design at Kingston University. 65, 120

EOOS is a design company working in three main areas of design: flagship stores, furniture and research. 96

Bruno Fattorini was born in 1939. He studied economics. In 1992 he took over the company MDF and began to implement an innovative and dynamic business and product strategy. 20, 126

Renzo Fauciglietti was born in Biella, Italy in 1941. He received a master's degree in industrial design and marketing from the Swiss STS technical school. In 1968 he founded the OK Studio with Graziella Bianchi; later, in 1989, Faucigletti was born, with the aim of contributing to design and research innovation as well as to the creation and design of new products. Faucigletti has received many national and international awards. 79

Chris Ferebee was born in 1971 Virginia Beach, USA, but has been based in New York since 1997. He is principal of the design studio 521 Design, which he formed with Laurice Parkin in 1999. He divides his time between painting, mixed media, photography, graphic and furniture design. 195

Christian Flindt is a Danish designer, whose work is about communication and social interaction, conditions between people and objects in a spatial environment. 34–5

The Forbo Flooring Design Studio is located in Assendelft, The Netherlands and is headed by industrial designer Josée de Pauw. 186–7

David Fowlkes studied at the Minneapolis College of Art and Design. He is the president and chief operating officer at Davin Wheels. He applies his design expertise to everything from concept to product launch. 190

Front is a design group based in Stockholm, Sweden. The members are Sofia Lagerkvist, Charlotte von der Lancken, Anna Lindgren and Katja Sävström. 207, 208

Stefano Gallizioli was born in Bergamo, Italy in 1964 and studied industrial design at the Polytechnic Institute of Milan. From 1987 to 1997 he worked in the practice of Antonio Citterio as a designer in charge of interiors and product design projects. In 1997 he opened his own practice in Milan, where he works with various manufacturing companies, such as Alivar, effetti, Frighetto and Fasem. In 2001 Gallizioli coordinated and created the image for a new brand, Coro, for whom he also designed the first product collection. 165

Christian Ghion was born in Montmorency, France in 1958. He graduated from Etude de Création Mobilier, Paris in 1987 and set up his own firm the following year, focusing on industrial and interior design for companies such as Trois Suisses, Neotu, Idee and Driade. 91

Stefano Giovannoni was born in in 1954 in La Spezia, Italy. He graduated in architecture in Florence in 1978 and now lives and works in Milan. Since 1979 he has been teaching and doing research at the the University of Florence Faculty of Architecture and has been Master-Professor at

the Domus Academy in Milan and at the Università del Progetto in Reggio Emilia. He also works as an industrial and interior designer and architect, specializing in plastic products. In 1991 he designed the Italian Pavilion at the exhibition 'Les Capitales Européennes du Nouveau Design' at the Centre Georges Pompidou in Paris. Giovannoni has won a number of awards and his works are part of the permanent archive of the Centre Georges Pompidou and of the Museum of Modern Art in New York. 16, 110, 183

Ulrich Goss, born in 1969, is a qualified toolmaker and studied industrial design at Fachhochschule Darmstadt University of Applied Science, Germany from 1992 to 1998. After a semester studying at San Jose State University, California, he completed an internship at n|p|k in The Netherlands. In 1999, he received the Neunkirchen Design Award for three of his designs. In 2000, he was credited with the Bavarian State Award for Young Designers. He founded his own company, gossindustrialdesign, in Darmstadt in 2001. 214

Konstantin Grcic was born in Munich, Germany in 1965. After training as a cabinetmaker at Parnham College in England, he studied design at the Royal College of Art, London (1998–90). Since setting up his own design practice, Konstantin Grcic Industrial Design, in Munich in 1991, he has developed furniture, products and lighting for some of Europe's leading design companies, including Authentics, Cappellini, Driade, Flos, littala, SCP and Whirlpool. Many of his products have received prestigious design awards: his 'Mayday-lamp', produced by Flos, was selected for inclusion in the permanent collection of the Museum of Modern Art in New York and won the Compasso d'Oro in 2001. 173, 215

Alfredo Häberli was born in 1964 in Buenos Aires, Argentina. He moved to Switzerland in 1977, where in 1991 he graduated in industrial design from the Höhere Schule für Gestaltung in Zurich. He received the Diploma Prize, SfGZ, in 1991. From 1988 onwards he worked in Zurich for the Museum für Gestaltung, where he was responsible for numerous exhibitions. In 1993 he set up his own studio, and subsequently worked for firms such as Alias, Authentics, Edra, Driade, Luceplan, Thonet and Zanotta. Recently Häberli has developed products for Asplund, Bd Ediciones de Diseño, Cappellini, Classicon, littala, Leitner, Moroso, Offecct and Rörstrand. Häberli's designs have been shown in numerous exhibitions throughout Europe and he has received many awards for his work. 141, 193

Ineke Hans was born in The Netherlands in 1966. She received an MA in furniture design from the Royal College of Art in London 1995. In 1998 she founded studio Ineke Hans/Arnhem. 28

degree in design from the Royal College of Art in London. In the early 1980s Lovegrove worked in Germany as a designer for Frog Design, on projects such as Sony Walkman and Apple Computers, before moving to Paris as a consultant to Knoll International, for whom he designed the highly successful Alessandri Office System. He was invited to join the Atelier de Nîmes – along with Jean Nouvel and Phillipe Stark – providing design consultancy for companies such as Cacharel, Louis Vuitton, Hermes and DuPont. Since he returned to London in 1988, his clients have included British Airways, Kartell, Cappellini, Idee, Moroso, Loom, Driade, Peugeot, Apple Computers, Olympus Cameras, Luceplan, Tag Heuer, Hackman, Japan Airlines and Toyo Ito Architects, Japan. His work has won numerous international awards, been extensively published and exhibited across the world and is held in the permanent collections of the Museum of Modern Art, New York and London's Design Museum. 71, 90–1

Bob Lucas is currently the head of a.i.t. design (adidas innovation team) in Portland, Oregon, USA. His most recent accomplishments include providing design direction for the new adidas '1' shoe, the first-ever running footwear product that can sense and adapt for any user on any terrain. Lucas, a graduate of San Jose State University with a BSc in industrial design, worked for Nike for more than 12 years before joining Adidas. 202–3

LUCY.D is a design studio based in Vienna, Austria that was founded by Barbara Ambrosz and Karin Stiglmair in 2003. It develops products, furniture and interiors, especially in the field of 'food and drink'. Lucy.D interprets many different aspects of culture, tradition and everyday life in their unconventional and emotional designs, which combine traditional and new materials. 105

Manuel Canovas is a French fabric house, renowned for its exquisite textiles and colours. The foundation of all the collections is the unique Manuel Canovas colour philosophy. Luxurious weaves and stunning prints are recognisable by their unusual colour harmonies. 196–7

Enzo Mari was born in Novara, Italy in 1932 and studied at the Academy of Fine Art in Milan. In 1963 he co-ordinated the Italian group Nuove Tendenze and in 1965 was responsible for the exhibition of optical, kinetic and programmed art at the Biennale in Zagreb. Mari is occupied with town planning and teaching and has organized courses for the history of art department at the University of Parma and the architecture department at the Polytechnic Institute of Milan. He has also lectured at various other institutions, including the Centre for Visual Communication in Parma and the Academy of Fine Arts in Carrara. He has been awarded the Compasso d'Oro several

times. His work is in the collections of various art museums, including the Stedelijk Museum in Amsterdam, the Musée des Arts Décoratifs in Paris and the Kunstmuseum in Düsseldorf. 215

Javier Mariscal opened the Mariscal Studio in 1990. He has recently inaugurated the Hotel Domine opposite the Guggenheim in Bilbao,Spain, in which he carried out an interior design project. He is currently undertaking a number of diverse graphic, audio-visual and editorial projects there. 41

Nani Marquina was born in Barcelona, Spain in 1952 and studied industrial design at the Massana school there. In 1986 she created her own brand in design and manufacture of rugs. 22, 107

Jason Martin studied industrial design at the Ohio State University, USA. He has been with Nike since 2000 working as a senior designer in the Timing and Techlab group where he has been responsible for the research, design and development of Nike's timing and monitoring product lines. He also creates conceptual design work for new business groups within Nike. Prior to joining Nike, Martin worked for Herbst Lazar and Bell in Chicago, specializing in the design and development of consumer and medical products. He has received international recognition for his work, which has won several awards and has been on display at the Smithsonian Cooper-Hewitt National Design Museum in New York City. 216–7

Ingo Maurer was born in 1932 on the Island of Reichenau, Lake Constance, Germany. He trained in typography in Germany and Switzerland and studied graphic design from 1954 to 1958. He started Design M in Munich in 1966 and received several design awards. His lamps have been exhibited internationally and are in the collections of various museums. 105

Max Factor is known as 'the make-up of make-up artists'. Max Factor himself was responsible for countless cosmetic innovations – from the first full-face foundation to false eyelashes –and the glamorous looks he created for Hollywood screen goddesses defined the concept of beauty in the twentieth century and were copied worldwide. 95

Alexander McQueen was born in London in 1969. Since leaving Saint Martins College of Art and Design in London, he has become one of the most famous fashion designers in the world. McQueen has been named 'British Designer of the Year' four times: in 1996, 1997, 2001 and 2003. 191

David Mellor trained as a silversmith and built his reputation as a designer of cutlery, which is manufactured at his factory in Sheffield, UK. Mellor was appointed Royal Designer for Industry and his

work can be seen in the Victoria & Albert Museum, London, the Worshipful Company of Goldsmiths and the Museum of Modern Art, New York. 20

Alessandro Mendini, architect, was born in Milan in 1931. He has edited the reviews *Casabella*, *Modo* and *Domus*. He works on products, furniture, interiors and installations for international firms such as Alessi, Philips, Swarovski and Swatch and acts as design consultant for various companies, including some in the Far East, directing image and design policies. Mendini is an honorary member of the Bezalel Academy of Art and Design in Jerusalem, has won the Compasso d'Oro Design Award, the Architectural League's Award in New York and is a Chevalier des Arts et des Lettres in France. In 1989, with his brother Francesco, he opened the Atelier Mendini in Milan. Work has included a tower block in Hiroshima, Japan and a number of buildings in Europe, including the Groningen Museum in The Netherlands and the Casino Arosa in Switzerland. Mendini's works are on display in various museums and private collections and his own work and that produced with the Atelier Alchimia have been the subject of monographic studies. 78, 151

Metz und Kindler Design was founded in 1995 by Guido Metz and Michael Kindler (both born in 1965) in the art-nouveau town of Darmstadt near Frankfurt in Germany. The studio works in public design for Mabeg and designs table tops for WMF, Auerhahn, Silit, Authentics and Flörke. Metz and Kindler have won many awards in Europe (red dots, if, design plus) and America (Good Design Chicago). 5, 17, 109

Miriam Mirri was born in Bologna, Italy in 1964 and now lives and works in Milan. Her clients include United Pets, Sigg and Alessi and Mandarina Duck. 94

Yujin Morisawa was born in Tokyo in 1975. He majored in industrial design at the University of the Arts in Philadelphia, Pennsylvania, USA. After working at Karim Rashid Inc., NY, USA, he joined Sony in 2002. He is now an art director of Sony Design Centre Tokyo office. 54–5

Ulf Moritz graduated as a textile designer from Krefelds Textilingenieurschule in Germany in 1960. He has been creating fabrics in his own design studio in Amsterdam for Sahco Hesslein since 1970. In 1986 he introduced his own fabric collection 'Ulf Moritz by Sahco Hesslein' to the market. His textile and interior design has been exhibited worldwide. 64, 88

Jasper Morrison was born in London in 1959. He studied design at Kingston Polytechnic and undertook postgraduate work at the Royal College of Art, London and the Hochschule der Kunste,

Berlin. In 1986 he set up his Office for Design in London, since when he has worked for Alessi, Alias, Cappellini, Flos, Magis, SCP, Rosenthal and Vitra. In 1995 his office was awarded the contract to design the new Hannover tram for Expo 2000. Recent projects have included furniture for the Tate Modern in London. 47, 49, 51, 127, 182–3, 184

Muji uses both in-house design teams and world-famous designers. Its policy of anonymity releases its products from associations and frees designers of their own trademark idiosyncrasies to produce work that is true to itself and the Muji concept. 108

Maxine Naylor is a furniture and lighting designer and Professor of Design at the University of Lincoln, England. Her award-winning and influential lighting design has been exhibited worldwide. Her research is concerned with the visual/cultural associations and implications of materials in the design process and outcome. Professor Naylor has taught at a number of highly distinguished universities in Europe and the USA. In 2000 she launched Studio Ball Art and Design with Ralph Ball and his brother, artist Keith Ball. 21

Newdealdesign, located in San Francisco, was founded to provide a personable alternative to the large product design franchises. Newdealdesign's award-winning designers have created products for leading brands, including Microsoft, Palm, Rio, Nike, Dell, Gateway, Sunbeam, MicronPC, ViewSonic, Fujitsu, SGI, News Corp and EMC. 133

Marc Newson's creations range from household objects, furniture, restaurants and watches to aircraft interiors. Australian-born Newson has won acclaim internationally, as well as a clientele that includes Flos, Cappellini, Magis, Nike, Alessi, Samsonite, Ideal Standard, Qantas and Ford. His works are in the collections of the Museum of Modern Art in New York, the Design Museum in London and the Musée National d'Art Moderne and the Centre Georges Pompidou in Paris. 57, 147

Nokia is committed to providing designs and user-interface solutions of the highest quality in product categories ranging from mobile devices to network elements and new market developments. 194

Johannes Norlander was born in Gothenburg, Sweden in 1974. He studied architecture at Chalmers University of Technology, Gothenburg (1993–95), graphic design and illustration at Konstfack University College of Arts, Crafts and Design in Stockholm (1996) and architecture at Stockholm Royal Institute of Technology (1996–9). In 2001 he formed his own design studio, Johannes Norlander Arkitektur and Form, in Stockholm and in 2003 he formed a production company, OJP, based in Austria. His clients include Box Design, B&B Italia, Asplund and Nola. 173

Jean Nouvel, architect and planner, was born in France in 1945 and opened his own architectural practice in 1970. For his work he has won, among other awards, the Gold Medal of the French Academy of Architecture, the Royal Gold Medal of the Royal Institute of British Architects, the Aga Khan Prize for the Arab World Institute, honorary fellowships in the RIBA and the AIA, France's National Grand Prize for Architecture, and, in 2001, Italy's Borromini Prize (for the Lucerne Culture and Congress Centre) and Japan's Praemium Imperial Career Prize. 172

Nuf design was founded in 2000 by Yeon Soo Son and Yoyo Wong, who met at Parsons School of Design in New York. Since then they have designed furniture and lighting and created several interiors in New York and Shanghai. 119

Nya nordiska is a renowned textile company in Germany, founded by Heinz Röntgen in 1964. Nya nordiska has won a large number of international design awards. 24, 25

Ora-Ïto is a multi-disciplinary creation studio with four main points of approach: design, multimedia, architectural design and communication. 152

Charlotte Perriand, 1903–99, was one of the most influential furniture designers of the early Modern Movement. 228–9

Florian Petri was born in 1973 in Darmstadt, Germany and studied industrial design there at the Fachhochschule from 1997 to 2002. He has collaborated with Möbelbau Kaether & Weise GmbH in Lamspringe, Germany since 2003. 46

Jordi Pigem de Palol was born in Spain in 1968. In 1997 he graduated in interior design from the School of Art Vic. His designs have been exhibited, awarded and published internationally.134–5

Bertjan Pot was born in Nieuwleusen, The Netherlands in 1975 and studied at the Design Academy Eindhoven. In 1998 he started working as a freelance designer and in 1999 co-founded Monkey Boys with Daniel White. In 2003 they decided to concentrate on their own projects and Pot was a guest teacher at the Academy of Arts Gerrit Rietveld in Amsterdam and the winner of the Material Fund Prize 2003 with his 'Random' chair. His work is in the collections of the Victoria & Albert Museum, London and the Museum Booijmans Van Beuningen, Rotterdam. His designs have been exhibited frequently since 2000. 177

Radi Designers was founded in 1992 in Paris. The group works in diverse fields and clients include Air France, Cartier and the City Hall of Paris. Radi Designers presented its first solo exhibition at the

Emmanuel Perrotin gallery in 1998 and in 2000 was voted 'Designer of the year' by the Salon du meuble de Paris. In 2001 Sandra Gering gallery in New York presented the group's work for the first time in the USA. The group members are Laurent Massaloux, Olivier Sidet and Robert Stadler. 117

Karim Rashid, who is half English, half Egyptian, was born in Cairo, Egypt in 1960 and raised mostly in Canada. He studied industrial design at Carleton University in Ottawa and pursued graduate design studies in Naples with Ettore Sottsass and others before moving to Milan to spend a year at the Rodolfo Bonetto Studio. He then worked for seven years with KAN Industrial Designers in Canada – while there co-founding and designing the Babel Fashion Collection and North – before opening his own practice in New York City in 1993. Rashid has worked for numerous clients globally, won many awards for products, packaging and restaurant interiors, and has more than 70 objects in permanent collections. His design work has been exhibited at major museums and galleries throughout North America and in London, Milan, Hamburg, Seoul, Tokyo, Austria and The Netherlands. Rashid has been a juror for several international competitions, a contributing writer to design periodicals andwas a full-time associate professor in industrial design for ten years at the University of the Arts in Philadelphia, the Pratt Institute in New York, Rhode Island School of Design, and the Ontario College of Art. He lectures internationally. 29, 57, 82–3

Giuseppe Rivadossi, who is a highly expressive artist in wood, designed the Custodie collection for Numa. These true sculptures in wood are formed using ancient methods, following the grain of the wood. Rivadossi uses Italian walnut (*Juglans regia*) from the foothills of the Alps in Italy, an area he knows well. 40

Hannes Rohringer was born in Austria, studied at the University of Applied Arts in Vienna and now lives and works as a designer and artist in Seewalchen and Vienna. In 1989 he founded Artium studio, which is dedicated to architecture, product design and applied arts. His designs are in the Folke Museum, Bremen, and the Museum of Applied Arts, Cologne, in Germany. His industrial customers include Santora-Santora Espresso, Lenzing AG, M-Group, ÖSPAG, Laufen-Duravit, Miele, Porche Design, Molto Luce and Schneider + Fichtel. Rohringer has won numerous prizes and has exhibited in Austria and abroad. 90

Francesco Rota was born in Milan in 1966. In 1994 he gained a bachelor's degree in product design from Art Center College of Design in La Tour Peliz, Switzerland and a year later he started his own design office in Milan. 18–19

Michael Rowe was born in High Wycombe, England in 1948. He graduated from the RCA in 1972 and set up his own silver and metalworking studio the same year. He has exhibited widely and is the recipient of many awards including the Sothebys Decorative Arts Award (1988), a Japan Foundation Artist's Fellowship (1993) and the Golden Ring of Honour from the German Association of Goldsmiths (2002). He is a Freeman of the Worshipful Company of Goldsmiths. Rowe is co-author with Richard Hughes of the seminal book *The Colouring, Bronzing and Patination of Metals*. Since 1984 he has been senior tutor in the department of metalwork and jewellery at the Royal College of Art. His work is in many public collections and a major retrospective exhibition of his work, organized by Birmingham Museum and Art Gallery, is touring internationally 2003–05. 76

Royal Mosa is a Dutch manufacturer of ceramic tiles. Royal Mosa has a huge range of tiles in a great many sizes, colours and designs for interior and exterior use. The factories in Maastricht produce five million square metres of wall and floor tiles per year, destined for Europe, North America, the Middle East and Asia. Royal Mosa works closely with architects and interior designers to develop new tiles and execute building projects. 106, 212

Masatoshi Sakaegi was born in the Chiba prefecture, Japan in 1944. In 1983 he founded his studio, which specializes in ceramic and plastic design and ceramic sculpture. In 1997 he showed his work at the 50th 'Premio Faenza', the international exhibition of contemporary ceramics in Faenza, Italy. 91, 134

Jaime Salm was born in Colombia in1978 and studied at the University of Arts in Philadelphia in the USA. Following his graduation, he founded Mio, a design laboratory dedicated to exploring sustainable furnishings for urban dwellers. 48

Barbara Schmidt was born in Berlin, Germany in 1967. She studied at the University College of Art and Design Halle, Germany and at the University of Art and Design Helsinki, Finland. She has been designing for Kahla/Thüringen Porzellan GmbH since 1991. 103

Scholten & Baijings consists of Stefan Scholten and Carole Baijings. Their designs have been exhibited and published many times. 168

Héctor Serrano was born in Valencia, Spain in 1974. After graduating from the ESDI CEU of Valencia he moved to London to study on the MA Design Products course at the Royal College of Art. He began collaboration with the Dutch firm Droog Design and his 'Superpatata' lamp is part of its collection. In the same year, he received the

Peugeot Design Award 2000 and since then his work has been featured in many publications. Serrano's work has also been exhibited in Milan, Frankfurt, Munich and New York and is in the collections of several museums. Having worked for various design studios, Serrano now works in London on new projects and exhibitions. 144

Michael Sieger is an internationally acclaimed photographer, graphic designer, trade-fair designer and creator. He was born in 1968 and studied industrial design at Essen Polytechnic and at the Münster University for Applied Sciences in Germany. Early in 2003, he established Sieger Design GmbH & Co. KG, in which he is a managing partner, with his brother Christian. The company focuses on industrial design and architecture, design management and graphic design, public relations and marketing. 166–7

Matthew Sindall is a British designer based in Paris. Born in 1958, he studied at Kingston Polytechnic, England, and has been working as a freelance designer since 1995. His clients include Sawaya & Moroni, Eclatec, Guinot, Peninsula group, Carré noir, Trois Suisses, Banque de Luxembourg, SNCF, Sunlight, Renault, Michelin and Groupe Richemont. 210–11

Hartmut Sinkwitz was born in Fredeburg/Hochsauerland, Germany in 1966 and studied industrial design at Comprehensive University Wuppertal. He has been the Head of design at Smart GmbH since 2000. 30–1

Paul Smith showed his first menswear collection in Paris in 1976 under the Paul Smith label. Today there are 12 different collections. Designed in Nottingham and London, the Paul Smith collections are primarily produced in England and Italy while the fabrics used are mainly of Italian, French and British origin. In 2002 Paul Smith collaborated with Cappellini to create the Mondo collection of furniture. Paul Smith is global – the collection is wholesaled to 35 countries and has 14 shops in England as well as shops in London, Nottingham, Paris, Milan, New York, Hong Kong, Singapore, Taiwan, the Philippines, Korea, Kuwait, U.A.E. – and more than 200 throughout Japan. Paul Smith himself remains fully involved in the Japanese business, designing clothes, choosing fabrics, approving shop locations and overseeing every development within the company. 185

Wieki Somers was born in in 1976 and studied at the Design Academy Eindhoven in The Netherlands (1995–2000). Her designs have been exhibited and awarded many times. 162–3

Speziell Produktgestaltung was founded in 2002 in Offenbach, Germany by Sybille Fleckenstein, Jens Pohlmann and Thilo Schwer. 103

Robert Stadler was born in Vienna. He studied design at the Istituto Europeo di Design in Milan and then at the Ecole Nationale Supérieure de Création Industrielle/Les Ateliers in Paris, where he co-founded the Radi Designers group in 1992. Since 2000 he has also worked independently. In 2002 he received a grant to spend six months in Rio de Janeiro. His clients include ACME, Magis and Swarovski and he has exhibited at the Espace Paul Ricard, Fondation Cartier and ToolsGalerie in Paris and at Klausengelhorn22 gallery, Vienna. 136

Philippe Starck was born in Paris in 1949 and trained at the Ecole Camondo in Paris. He has been responsible for interior design schemes for Francois Mitterand's apartment and multi-purpose buildings such as the offices of Asahi Beer in Tokyo. As a product designer he collaborates with Alessi, Baum, Driade, Flos, Kartell and Vuitton. From 1993 to 1996 he was worldwide artistic director for the Thomson Consumer Electronics Group. In 1999–2000 he finished two central London hotels for the Ian Schrager group. 116, 130–1

Peter Struycken, born in The Hague, The Netherlands in 1939, is a visual artist specializing in relationships between colours. 186–7

Studio Job is well known for a refined play of visual clues and its work crosses boundaries between design and autonomous art. Gallery Dilmos and Royal Tichelaar Makkum in The Netherlands are both showing part of Studio Job's 'story' this year. 176–7

Taku Sugawara was born in Tokyo in 1969 and majored in product design at Tama Art University. He joined Sony in 1996 and is now art director at Sony Design Centre Tokyo office. 124–5

Yuka Takeda was born in Shizuoka, Japan in 1962. She majored in Visual Communication Design at Musashino Art University before joining Sony in 1985. She now works as producer at Sony Design Centre Tokyo office. 124–5

Mats Theselius was born in Stockholm, Sweden in 1956. He studied industrial design and small-scale architecture at Konstfack University College of Arts, Crafts and Design in Stockholm from 1979 to 1984. His designs have been awarded many times and exhibited worldwide. 184

Timorous Beasties was established in 1990 by Paul Simmons and Alistair McAuley, who met at Glasgow School of Art in the 1980s. The company name is taken from a line in Robert Burn's poem 'To a Mouse' (pronounced 'Moose'). The work of the pair, who have been described by *Blueprint* magazine as 'Textile Mavericks', crosses many disciplines and styles. 38–9

Scott Tomlinson is currently a senior industrial designer in a.i.t. (adidas innovation team) with Adidas in Portland, Oregon, USA. His most recent accomplishments include the hardware design for the new Adidas '1' shoe, an industry breakthrough. Prior to joining Adidas, Tomlinson worked at Ziba, where he won several national awards including a Gold IDSA (for the M-Systems Flash memory Key) in 2000. He has worked in the areas of consumer electronics, industrial equipment, contract furniture, interior furniture systems, consumer goods and performance footwear. Central to his work is the idea of developing familiar interactions with new technologies, new functions and new use scenarios. Scott graduated from the University of Northumbria at Newcastle, England, with a first-class honors BA degree in industrial design in 1997. 202–3

Peter Traag was born in 1979 in Tegelen, The Netherlands. He studied design at the Hogeschool voor de Kunsten, Arnhem and the Royal College of Art, London from 1997 to 2001. 174

Jun Uchiyama was born in Tokyo in 1961 and majored in science and engineering at Waseda University in Tokyo. He joined Sony in 1986. 124–5

Paolo Ulian was born in Massa-Carrara, Italy in 1961. He studied painting at the Academy of Fine Art in Carrara and industrial design at the I.S.I.A. in Florence. His work has been shown in numerous exhibitions worldwide and he collaborates with companies including Driade, Indarte, View , Sensi&C.,Progetti , Fontana Arte, Seccose, Luminara, BBB Emmebonacina and Zani & Zani. 36

Patricia Urquiola was born in Oviedo, Spain and graduated from the Faculty of Architecture of Madrid Polytechnic in 1989. In 1996 she became head of the Lissoni Associati design group, working for Alessi, Antares-Flos, Artelano, Boffi, Cappellini, Cassina, Kartell and others. She has also designed independently for B&B, Bosa, De Vecchi, Fasem, Kartell, Liv'it, MDF Italia, Molteni & C., Moroso and Tronconi, as well as designing stands and showrooms for Knoll, Moroso, Sag 80 and Somma. In 2001 she was chair of the jury for the nineteenth CDIM Design Award and a lecturer on the exhibition design course of Domus Academy, Milan. She now works in design, exhibitions, art direction and architecture from her Milan studio. 74–5, 157

Vincent Van Duysen was born in Lokeren, Belgium in 1962 and studied architecture at the Higher Institute of Architecture St. Lucas in Gent. In 1990 he opened his own studio in Antwerp. He has completed many projects for interiors, single-family homes, office spaces and shops across Europe and in the USA and Tokyo and also designs furniture and lighting for firms such as Obumex,

B&B Italia, Modular and Appart. His work has been featured in many books, magazines and exhibitions worldwide. 104–5

Kiki van Eijk was born in Tegelen, The Netherlands in 1978. She studied at the Design Academy Eindhoven, graduating in 2000. Her designs have been exhibited in The Netherlands, Italy, UK and Germany. 69, 201

Edward Van Vliet runs SEVV (Studio Edward Van Vliet), a multi-disciplinary design studio offering complete design solutions for both residential and commercial markets. In the realization of projects, SEVV strives for balance between touch, atmosphere and emotion. This is combined with high-quality product standards, multi-functionality and a startling use of materials. SEVV is specialized in luxurious and 'image-distinctive' products and interiors for several leading international companies. The studio's wide variety of assignments ranges from watches to restaurants. In addition, SEVV designs and produces its own range of furniture and lighting products. 40

Roderick Vos was born in The Netherlands in 1965 and studied industrial design in Eindhoven. He worked for Kenji Ekuans GK in Tokyo and Ingo Maurer in Munich before co-founding a studio, Studio Maupertuus, with Claire Vos-Teeuwen. Their clients include Espaces et Lignes, Driade, Authentics and Alessi and their work has been shown at the Milan, Cologne and New York Furniture Fairs. 157

Bernard Vuarnesson was born in Paris in1935. After studying engineering at the Ecole Supérieure du Bois in Paris, he spent one year training at the Royal Forestry School in Stockholm, Sweden. In 1966 he obtained a degree as an engineer in Conservatoire National des Arts et Métiers in Paris, then managed the engineering office for the design of wooden roof trusses following the American 'Gang Nail' system. In 1972, together with his wife Ariane, he launched the Société Sculptures-Jeux for the design of playground equipment for unsupervised areas. Sculptures-Jeux has participated in playground exhibitions in France, Germany and Switzerland. In 1982 they began designing objects and furniture. 132

Nobert Wangen was born in 1962 in Prum, Germany and served a carpenter's apprenticeship before studying sculpture and architecture in Dusseldorf, Aachen and Munich. In 1991 he graduated in architecture from the Technical University in Munich and worked as a set designer. In 1995 his folding armchair 'Atilla' was selected for the show 'Die Neue Sammlung Munchen'; it was subsequently acquired for the Vitra Design Museum in Weil am Rhein. 37

Hannes Wettstein was born in Ascona, Switzerland in 1958. Since 1991 he has been teaching in tandem with his professional activities, first as lecturer at the Swiss Federal Institute of Technology, Zürich and then as professor at the Karlsruhe Hochschule für Gestaltung. In addition to furniture and furnishing accessories, he designs professional audio equipment and watches. His clients include Baleri, Cassina and Bulo. 68

Hans Weyers and Klaas Borms have been working together for 12 years. They have exhibited in Amsterdam, Paris, Milan, Lubljana, New York, Barcelona, Cologne, Brussels and Antwerp. In 2002 they were awarded at the International Composites Design Competition for their biodegradable composite coffin 'Gravioli'. 83

John Whiteman is currently a footwear designer in a.i.t. (adidas innovation team) in Portland, Oregon, USA, where he started work as an intern in the summer of 2002. His most recent accomplishments include upper and outsole design for the adidas '1' shoe, the first-ever intelligent running shoe. Whiteman is originally from St. Louis, Missouri and attended Carnegie Mellon University in Pittsburgh, Pennsylvania, from where he graduated with a BFA in industrial design in 2002. 202–3

Scott Wilson was born in 1969. He graduated from Rochester Institute of Technology in New York, where he received his degree in industrial, interior and packaging design in 1991. He went on to work at IDEO, and in 1999, he founded MOD, a virtual design team (www.studiomod.com). In 2001, he joined Nike as creative director of its sport's technology group, creating franchise products such as the 'Presto' digital bracelet and the Oregon Series watch collection (which Lance Armstrong has used for consecutive Tour de France victories). Currently he is a global creative director for Nike's Explore group, an advance development group focused on new business opportunities, partnerships and technologies. He also collaborates with companies such as JOLT Lighting, Quinze&Milan (Belgium), OMA and Moroso on various projects, from lighting to contract and residential furniture systems. 216–7

Stephanie Ziegler was born in 1976 in Munich and studied industrial design in Darmstadt from 1996 to 2001. Following an internship at vogt+weizenegger in Berlin, she spent a semester studying abroad at the Instituto Europeo di Design in Milan. She was presented with the Braun Award for her 'Carving Sled' design in 1998. She has been working with Ulrich Goss at gossindustrialdesign in Darmstadt since 2001 and graduated with a Master of Arts degree in communication management from the University of Pforzheim, Germany in 2003. 214

Suppliers

Page 16 Alessi SpA, 6 Via Privata Alessi, 28882 Crusinallo, Verbania, Italy T.+39 0323 868611 F.+39 0323 641709 E. info@alessi.com W. www.alessi.com

Page 17 WMF Aktiengesellschaft, Eberhardstraße, 73309 Geislingen, Germany T.+49 (0)73 31251 F.+49 (0)73 3145387 W. www.wmf.de

Pages 18–19 Paola Lenti srl, Via XX Settembre 7, 20036 Meda (MI), Italy T.+39 0362 343216 F.+39 0362 70492 E. info@paolalenti.it W. www.paolalenti.it

Page 20 MDF Italia srl, Via Morimondo 5/7, 20143 Milan, Italy T.+39 02 81804100 F.+39 02 81804108 E. infomdf@mdfitalia.it W. www.mdfitalia.it

David Mellor Design Ltd, The round building, Hathersage, S32 1BA, UK T.+44 (0)1433 650220 F.+44 (0)1433 650944 E. davidmellor@ukonline.co.uk

Page 21 Studio Ball, 177 Waller Road, London SE14 5LX, UK T.+44 (0)20 72071360 F.+44 (0)20 75147109 E. info@studioball.co.uk W. www.studioball.co.uk

Page 22 Nanimarquina, Església 4-6, 08024 Barcelona, Spain T.+34 932 376465 F.+34 932 175774 E. info@nanimarquina.com W. www.nanimarquina.com

Page 23 The Gallery Mourmans, Keizer Karelplein 8B, 6211 TC Maastricht, The Netherlands T.+31 (0)43 3260477 F.+31 (0)43 3260004

Pages 24–5 Nya nordiska textiles GmbH, An den Ratswiesen, 29451 Dannenberg, Germany T.+49 (0)5861 80943 F.+49 (0)5861 80912 E. secretary@nya.com W. www.nya.com

Page 26 Klay, Viale Coni Zugna 23, 20144 Milan, Italy T:+39 0348 7040559 F.+39 02 462067 E. info@klayonline.com

Page 27 Corp. Modular works, 716-16 Negiuchi Matsudo City, Chiba, 270-0011 Japan T.+81 (0)47 3471638 F.+81 (0)47 3471638

Page 28 Ineke Hans/Arnhem, Dijkstraat 105/107, 6828 JS Arnhem, The Netherlands T.+31 (0)26 3893892 F.+31 (0)26 4459950 E. info@inekehans.com W. www.inekehans.com

Page 29 Bozart, 320 Race St, Philadelphia, PA 19106, USA T.+1 (0)215 6272223 F.+1 (0)215 6272218 E. info@bozart.com W. www.bozart.com

Pages 30–1 Smart GmbH, Leibnizstraße 2, 71032 Böblingen, Germany W. www.smart.com

Pages 32–3 Inflate Design Ltd, 28 Exmouth Market, London, EC1R 4QE, UK T.+44 (0)20 77139096 F.+44 (0)20 77139394 E. info@inflate.co.uk W. www.inflate.co.uk

Pages 34–5 Christian Flindt, Warsaaesvej 14, 3TH, 1972 Copenhagen, Denmark T.+45 (0)26709918 E: flindt@flindtdesign.dk W. www.flindtdesign.dk

Page 36 Paolo Ulian, Via Silvio Pellico 4, 54100 Massa (MS), Italy T.+39 0585 253573 F.+39 0585 253573 E. drugos@iol.it

Page 37 Boffi SpA, Via Oberdan 70, 20030 Lentate sul Seveso (MI), Italy T.+39 0362 5341 F.+39 0362 565077 E. info@boffi.com W. www.boffi.com

Pages 38–9 Timorous Beasties, 7 Craigend Place, Glasgow, G13 2UN, UK T.+44 (0)141 9593331 F.+44 (0)141 9598880 E. info@timorousbeasties.com W. www.timorousbeasties.com

Page 40 Numa/Serafino Zani, Via Zanagnolo 17b, 25066 Lumezzane Gazzolo (Brescia), Italy T.+39 030 871861 F.+39 030 8970620 E. numa@serafinozani.it W. www.serafinozani.it

Moooi, Jacob Catskade 35, 1052 BT Amsterdam, The Netherlands T.+31 (0)20 6815051 F.+31 (0)20 6815056 E. info@moooi.com W. www.moooi.com

Page 41 Nanimarquina, *see page 22*

Page 42 Magis SpA, Via Magnodola 15, 31045 Motta Di Livenza, Treviso, Italy T.+39 0422 862600 F.+39 0422 766395 E. info@magisdesign.com W. www.magisdesign.com

Pages 42–3 Maharam, 251 Park Avenue South, New York, NY 10010, USA T.+1 8006453943 E. clientservices@maharam.com W. www.maharam.com

Pages 44–5 Zoltan Gruppo De Padova, Via Benedetto Croce 8, 20090 Vimodrone, (MI), Italy T.+39 02 27400160 F.+39 02 27400184 E. safe@zoltan.it W. www.zoltan.it

Page 46 Möbelbau Kaether & Weise GmbH, Dammstraße 43, 31195 Lamspringe, Germany T.+49 (0)5183 677 F.+49 (0)5183 2766 E. info@kaetherundweise.de W. www.kaetherundweise.de

Page 47 Rowenta UK, Groupe Seb UK Ltd, 11–49 Station Road, Langley SL3 8DR, UK T.+44 (0)845 6021454 E. customerrelations@rowenta.co.uk W. www.rowenta.co.uk

Page 48 Mio Company LLC, 1234 Hamilton Street 2D, Philadelphia, PA 19123, USA T.+1 215 6810909 F.+1 215 9259359 E. info@mioculture.com www.mioculture.com

Page 49 Rowenta UK, *see page 47*

Page 50 Kartell SpA, Via delle Industrie 1, 20082 Noviglio (MI), Italy T.+39 02 900121 F.+39 02 90091212 E. kartell@kartell.it W. www.kartell.it

Page 51 Rowenta UK, *see page 47*

Pages 52–3 Debbie Jane Buchan, 9 Peel Street, Macclesfield, SK11 8BH, UK T.+44 (0)1625 501671 E. debbiejanemagee@hotmail.com

Pages 54–5 Sony Corporation, 6-7-35 Kitashinagawa Shinagawa-ku, 141-0001 Tokyo, Japan T.+81 3 5448 6780 F.+81 3 5448 7823 E. hisayo@dc.sony.co.jp W. www.sony.co.jp

Page 56 Chris Kabel Designs, Blommersdijkselaan 3b, 3036 NA Rotterdam, The Netherlands T.+31 (0)6 19186064 E. mail@chriskabel.com W. www.chriskabel.com

Page 57 Artemide, Via Bergamo 18, 20010 Pregnana (MI), Italy T.+39 02 93518235 F.+39 02 93518370 E. dtd@artemide.cm W. www.artemide.com

Alessi SpA, *see page 16*

Page 58 Swarovski Austria, Pradler Straße 78, 6023 Innsbruck, Austria T.+43 512 33488141 F.+43 512 3348843 E. customer_relations.at@swarovski.com W. www.swarovski.com

Page 59 WMF Aktiengesellschaft, *see page 17*

Pages 60–1 Magis SpA, *see page 42*

Pages 62–3 Teamwork srl, Via Fontana 21, 42048 Rubiera (RE), Italy T.+39 0522 621332 F.+39 0522 260140 E. info@teamworkitaly.com W. www.teamworkitaly.com

Page 63 Andreu World S.A, C. Los Sauces 7, Urb.Olimar, 46370 Chiva, Valencia, Spain T.+34 (0)961 805355 F.+34 (0)961 805305 E. aworld@andreuworld.com W. www.andreuworld.com

Page 64 Sahco, Kreuzburger str. 17-19, 90471 Nürnberg, Germany T.+49 (0)911 99870124 F.+49 (0)911 9987480 E. info@sahco-hesslein.com W. www.sahco-hesslein.com

Page 65 El Ultimo Grito, 4 Peacock Yard, Iliffe Street, London, SE17 3LH, UK T.+44 (0)20 77039939 F.+44 (0)20 77039939 E. info@elultimogrito.co.uk W. www.elultimogrito.co.uk

Page 66 M-Pro, Hirosawa 1-1-102, Kariya, Aichi, 448-0001, Japan T.+81 566 26 2669 F.+81 566 26 2669 E. ido@auecc.aichi-edu.ac.jp

Page 67 Debbie Jane Buchan, *see pages 52–3*

Page 68 Bulo, Industriezone Noord B6, 2800 Mechelen, Belgium T.+32 (0)15 282828 F.+32 (0)15 282829 E. info@bulo.be W. www.bulo.com

Page 69 Kiki van Eijk, Kromakkerweg 3, 5616 SB Eindhoven, The Netherlands T.+31 06 41361870 E. info@kikiworld.nl W. www.kikiworld.nl

Page 70 Sachio Hihara Industrial Design Office, 1-5-6 Shintori, Shizuoka 420-0065, Japan T.+81 (0)54 6520057 F.+81 (0)54 6520058 E. hihara@sachio.jp W. www.sachio.jp

Page 71 Tag Heuer SA, 14A Avenue des Champs Montants, 2074 Marin, Switzerland T.+41 32 7556000 F.+41 32 7556400 W. www.tagheuer.com

Pages 72–3 The Gallery Mourmans, *see page 23*

Pages 74–5 Moroso SpA, Via Nazionale 60, 33010 Cavalicco, Udine, Italy T.+39 0432 577111 F.+39 0432 570761 E. info@moroso.it W. www.moroso.it

Page 76 Michael Rowe, c/o Royal College of Art, Kensington Gore, London, SW7 2EU, UK T.+44 (0)20 75904263 E. m.rowe@rca.ac.uk

Pages 76–7 Studio Tord Boontje, The Bake House, Basing Court, 16a Peckham High Street, London, SE15 5DT, UK T.+44 (0)20 77326460 F.+44 (0)20 77326460 E. info@tordboontje.com W. www.tordboontje.com

Page 78 Alessi SpA, *see page 16*

Page 79 Segis SpA, Via Umbria 14, 53036 Poggibonsi (SI), Italy T.+39 0577 980333 F.+39 0577 938090 E. segis@segis.it W. www.segis.it

Pages 80–1 Runtal, Zehnder Group, Moortalstraße 1, 5722 Graenichen, Switzerland T.+41 62 8551546 F.+41 62 8551544

Pages 82–3 For the dogs, 2 Silver Ave, Toronto, Ontario, M6R 3A2, Canada T.+1 (0)866 4066966 E. info@forthedogs.com W. www.forthedogs.com

Edra SpA, PO Box 28, 56030 Perignano (PI), Italy T.+39 0587 616660 F.+39 0587 617500 E. edra@edra.com W. www.edra.com

Page 84–5 Design Centre Canon Inc, 3-30-2 Simomaru, Shimomaruko, Ohta-Ku, 146-8501 Tokyo, Japan. T.+81 3 3758 2111 F.+81 3 5482 8272 W. www.canon.com

Page 85 Kate Hume Glass, Kerksraat 152, 1017GR Amsterdam, The Netherlands T.+31 (0)20 6253522 F.+31 (0)20 4205750 E. kate.hume@euronet.nl

Pages 86–7 Dodo Arslan, P.za della Repubblica 5, 20121 Milan, Italy T.+39 02 36533352 E. dodo@arslan.it W. www.arslan.it

Page 88 Sahco, *see page 64*

Page 89 Maharam, *see pages 42–3*

Page 90 Streitner GmbH Ipftal 1, 4491 Niederneukirchen, Austria T.+43 (0)7224 7385 F.+43 (0)7224 7404 E. office@streitner.at W. www.streitner.at

Page 91 Driade SpA, Via Padana Inferiore 12, 29012 Fossadello di Caorso (PC), Italy T.+39 0523 818618 F.+39 0523 822628 E. com.it@driade.com W. www.driade.com

Sakaegi design studio 1-74 Nakamizuno-cho, 489-0005 Seto-shi, Aichi-ken, Japan T.+81 (0)561 483991 F.+81 (0)561 483991 E. sakaegi103@yahoo.co.jp

Pages 92–3 Ross Lovegrove, Studio X, 21 Powis Mews, London, W11 1JN, UK T.+44 (0)20 72297104 F.+44 (0)20 72297032 E. studiox@compuserve.com

Page 94 Alessi SpA, *see page 16*

Page 95 www.maxfactor.com

Worldwide Co, UK T.+44 (0)20 87352882 F.+44 (0)20 87352999 W. www.npw.co.uk

Page 96 Walter Knoll, Bahnhofstraße 25, 71083 Herrenberg, Germany T.+49 (0)70 322080 F.+49 (0)70 32208250 E. info@walterknoll.de

Page 97 Whirlpool Eurpope srl, 1-21024 Biandronno, Localitá Cassinetta, Italy W. www.whirlpool.com

Page 98 Gubi, Grønnegade 10, 1107 Copenhagen, Denmark T. +45 33326368 F. +45 33326069 E. gubi@gubi.dk W. www.gubi.dk

Page 99 Debbie Jane Buchan, *see pages 52–3*

Pages 100–1 One Off, Fabbrica del Vapore, Via Luigi Nono 7, 20154 Milan, Italy T. +39 0236517890 F. +39 02342290 E. info@oneoffonline.com W. www.oneoffonline.com

Pages 102–3 Debbie Jane Buchan, *see pages 52–3*

Page 103 Kahla/Thüringen Porzellan GmbH, Christian Eckardt Str. 38, 07768 Kahla, Germany T. +49 3642479281 E. shr@kahlaporzellan.com W. www.kahlaporzellan.com

Pages 104 When objects work, T Molentje 11, 8300 Knokke, Belgium T. +32 (0)50 613354 F. +32 (0)50 340141 E. info@whenobjectswork.com W. www.whenobjectswork.com

Page 105 Swarovski, *see page 58*

Lucy. D, Hormayrgasse 7, 1170 Vienna, Austria T. +43 1 9248332 E. office@lucyd.com W. www.lucyd.com

Page 106 Royal Mosa, The Netherlands T. +31 (0)43 3689229 F. +31 (0)43 3689356 W. www.mosa.nl

Page 107 Nanimarquina, *see page 22*

Page 108 www.muji.co.uk

Page 109 WMF Aktiengesellschaft, *see page 17*

Apple Computer Inc, 1 Infinite Loop, Cupertino, CA 95014, USA T. +1 408 9749202 F. +1 408 2556955 W. www.apple.com

Pages 110 Fiat Auto, Corso Orbassano 367, 10137 Torino, Italy T. +39 011 0030670 F. +39 011 0033560 W. www.fiat.com

Page 111 Studio Tord Boontje, *see pages 76–7*

Pages 112–13 Debbie Jane Buchan, *see pages 52–3*

Page 113 Pallucco Italia SpA, Via Azzi, 3631040 Castagnole di Paese (TV), Italy T. +39 0422 438800 F. +39 0422 438555 E. infopallucco@palluccobellato.it W. www.pallucco.com

VIA, 29-35 Avenue Daumesnil, 75012 Paris, France T. +33 (0)1 46281111 F. +33 (0)1 46281313 E. via@mobilier.com W. www.via.asso.fr

Pages 114–15 Droog Design, 7a-7b Staalstraat, 1011 JJ Amsterdam, The Netherlands T. +31 020 5235050 F. +31 020 3201710 E. info@droogdesign.nl W. www.droogdesign.nl

Page 116 Oregon Scientific France, 3 Avenue Francis de Pressensé, 93200 Saint-Denis, France

T. +33 (0)1 55932688 F. +33 (0)1 55932699 E. info@oregonscientific.fr W. www.oregonscientific.fr

Page 117 Canividro, Zona Industrial da Marinha Grande, Rua de Portugal Lote 7, Ap 281, 2431 904 Marinha Grande, Portugal T. +351 244545130 F. +351 244 545139 E. design@canividro.pt W. www.canividro.pt

Page 118 Ebisukasei, Head office, Taiyo Center Bldg. 8F, 4-9-28 Nishinakajima, Yodogawa-Ku, Osaka, Japan T. +81 06 63012618 F. +81 06 63000947 E. info@ebisukasei.co.jp W. www.ebisukasei.co.jp/english/

Page 119 Nuf Design Inc, 2 Cornelia Street #506, New York, NY 10014 T. +1 212 6471517 F. +1 212 2430199 E. info@nufdesign.com W. www.nufdesign.com

Interior Crafts of the Islands, Inc, 3A General Maxilom Avenue, Cebu City 6000, Philippines T. +63 (0)917 6212121 F. +63 (0)32 2312555 E. kennethc@interiorcrafts.com.ph

Page 120 Nola Industrier AB, PO Box 17701, 11893 Stockholm, Sweden T. +46 (0)8 7021960 F. +46 (0)8 7021962 E. headoffice@nola.se W. www.nola.se

Page 121 Interior Crafts of the Islands, *see page 119*

Page 122 Chris Christou, Youmeus Design Ltd, 59 Nathans Road, Wembley, HA0 3RZ, UK T. +44 (0)20 89048117 E. mail@youmeusdesign.com W. www.youmeusdesign.com

Page 123 Shin & Tomoko Azumi, Unit 7, Haybridge House, 15 Mount Pleasant Hill, London, E5 9NB, UK T. +44 (0)20 88800031 F. +44 (0)20 88800697 E. mail@azumi.co.uk W. www.azumi.co.uk

Pages 124–5 Sony Corporation, *see page 54–5*

Page 126 MDF Italia srl, *see page 20*

Page 127 Cap Design SpA, Via Marconi 35, 22060 Arosio (CO), Italy T. +39 031 759111 F. +39 031 763322 E. cappellini@cappellini.it W. www.cappellini.it

Page 128 Segis SpA, *see page 79*

Page 129 Maharam, *see pages 42–3*

Pages 130–1 Cassina SpA, Via L. Busnelli 1, 20036 Meda (MI), Italy T. +39 03623721 F. +39 0362342246 E. info@cassina.it W. www.cassina.it

Page 132 Bellato Pallucco, Via Azzi 36, 31040 Castagnole di Laese (TV), Italy T. +39 04 22438511 F. +39 04 22438555

Page 133 Netgear Inc, T-4500 Great America Expressway, Santa Clara, CA 95054, USA T. +1 408 9078092 F. +1 408 9078097 W. www.netgear.com

Page 134 Sakaegi design studio, *see page 91*

Pages 134–5 Jordi Pigem de Palol, Ronda Ferran Puig 25 pal 4a, 17001 Girona (CAT), Spain T. +34 972 209735 F. +34 972 209735 E. pigem@intercomgi.com

Page 136 Coopa Roca, Rio de Janeiro, Brazil T. +55 21 22499463 F. +55 21 22499463 E. coopa-roca@coopa-roca.org.br W. www.coopa-roca.org.br

Page 137 Yves Béhar, Fuseproject, 123 South Park, San Francisco, CA 94107, USA T. +1 415 9081492 F. +1 415 9081491 W. www.fuseproject.com

Debbie Jane Buchan, *see pages 52–3*

Pages 138–9 Vitra AG, Klünenfeldstraße 22, 4127 Birsfelden, Switzerland T. +41 (0)61 377 0000 F. +41 (0)61 377 1720 E. info@vitra.com W. www.vitra.com

Page 140 Birkenstock, 8171 Redwood Blvd, Novato, CA 94945, USA T. +1 800 4879255 W. www.birkenstock.com

Page 141 ClassiCon GmbH, Sigmund-Riefler-Bogen 3, 81829 Munich, Germany T. +49 (0)89 748133-0 F. +49 (0)89 7809996 E. info@classicon.com W. www.classicon.com

Weyers & Borms, Kaaistraat 2, 9140 Tielrode, Belgium T. +32 3 7110517 F. +32 3 7111947 E. weyers.borms@busmail.net

Page 142 Santa & Cole S.A, Santissima Trinidad del Monte 10, 08017 Barcelona, Spain T. +34 93 8462437 F. +34 93 8711767 W. www.santacole.com

Page 143 Lapalma, Via Belladoro 25, 35010 Cadoganeghe, Padova, Italy T. +39 049 702788 F. +39 049 700889 E. info@lapalma.it W. www.lapalma.it

Maharam, *see pages 42–3*

Page 144 Metalarte S.A, Tambor del Bruc 10, 08970 Sant Joan Despi (Barcelona) Spain T. +34 93 4770069 F. +34 93 4770086 E. metalarte@metalarte.com W. www.metalarte.com

Page 145 Debbie Jane Buchan, *see pages 52–3*

Pages 146–7 Debbie Jane Buchan, *see pages 52–3*

Page 147 KDDI Corporation, Garden Air Tower, 10-10, Iidabashi 3-chome, Chiyoda-ku, Tokyo 102-8460, Japan T. +81 3 3347 0077 W. www.kddi.com

Pages 148–9 Isokon Plus, Turnham Green Terrace Mews, London W4 1QU, UK T. +44 (0)20 89940636 F. +44 (0)20 89945635 E. mail@isokonplus.com W. www.isokonplus.com

Pages 150–1 Maharam, *see pages 42–3*

Page 151 De Padova, Corso Venezia 14, 20121 Milan, Italy T. +39 02777201 F. +39 0277720270 E. press@depadova.it W. www.depadova.it

Pages 152 www.heineken.com

Pages 152–3 Debbie Jane Buchan, *see pages 52–3*

Pages 154–5 www.porsche.de

Page 156 Yoshiki Hishinuma Co, Ltd, 3-12-12-2F Higashi, Shibuya-ku, Tokyo, Japan T. +81 3 54640222

F. +81 3 54640505 E. info@yoshikihishinuma.co.jp W. www.yoshikihishinuma.co.jp

Page 157 Driade SpA, *see page 91*

Pages 158–9 Pallucco, *see page 113*

Pages 160–1 WMF Aktiengesellschaft, *see page 17*

Pages 162–3 European Ceramic Work Centre (EKWC), Zuid-Willemsvaart 215, 5211 SG Hertogenbosch, The Netherlands T. +31 (0)73 6124500 F. +31 (0)73 6124568 W. www.ekwc.nl

Page 164 Thonet GmbH, Michael Thonet Straße 1, 35066 Frankenberg, Germany T. +49 64 515080 F. +49 64 51508108 E. info@thonet.de W. www.thonet.de

Lorenzo Damiani, Via Segantini 55, 20035 Lissone (MI), Italy E. Lorenzo.damiani@tin.it

Page 165 Coro, Via Cavallotti 53, 20052 Monza, Italy T. +39 039 2726260 F. +39 039 2727409 E. info@coroitalia.com W. www.coroitalia.com

Pages 166–7 United Labels AG, Gildenstr. 6, 48157 Münster, Germany T. +49 (0)251 32210 F. +49 (0)251 3221999 E. info@unitedlabels.com W. www.unitedlabels.com

Page 167 Buenavista Datacasting, 500 S. Buena Vista Dr, Burbank, CA 91521, USA

Page 168 Scholten and Baijings, Sandvikweg 2-B, 1013 BA Amsterdam, The Netherlands T. +31 (0)20 4208940 F. +31 (0)20 4208941 E. info@scholtenbaijings.com W. www.scholtenbaijings.com

Pages 168–9 Design Gallery Milano, Italy T. +39 02 36520950 F. +39 02 43916241 E. info@designgallerymilano.com W. www.designgallerymilano.com

Pages 170–1 Boffi SpA, *see page 37*

Page 172 Kvadrat A/S, Lundbergsvej 10, 8400 Ebeltoft Denmark T. +45 89 531866 F. +45 89 531800 E. kvadrat@kvadrat.dk W. www.kvadrat.dk

Page 173 Moroso SpA, *see page 74–5*

Nola Industrier AB, *see page 120*

Page 174 Edra SpA, *see pages 82–3*

Page 175 Moooi, *see page 40*

Pages 176–7 Nederlands Textielmuseum, Goirkestraat 96, 5046 GN Tilburg, The Netherlands T. +31 (0)13 5367475 F. +31 (0)13 5363240 E. textielmuseum@tilburg.nl W. www.tilburg.nl/textielmuseum

Page 178 Burberry, 10 St Albans Street, London, SW1Y 4SQ, UK W. www.burberry.com

Page 179 Ycami SpA, Via Provinciale 31–33, 22060 Novedrate (Como), Italy T. +39 031 7897311 F. +39 031 7897350 E. info@ycami.com W. www.ycami.com

240

Picture credits

Pages 180–1 and 182 Cap Design SpA, *see* page 127

Page 183 Rubinetteria Webert srl, Via Maria F. Beltrani, 28014 Maggiora (NO), Italy T. +39 0322 870810 F. +39 0322 87472 E. info@webert.it W. www.webert.it

Magis SpA, *see* page 42

Page 184 Maharam, *see* pages 42–3

Källemo AB, Box 605 331 26, Värnamo, Sweden T. +46 (0)370 15000 F. +46 (0)370 15060 E. info@kallemo.se W. www.kallemo.se

Page 185 Maharam, *see* pages 42–3

Pages 186–7 Forbo Linoleum B.V, P.O. Box 13, 1560 AA Krommenie, The Netherlands T. +31 75 6477477 F. +31 75 6477701 E. contact@forbo.com W. www.forbo.com

Pages 188 Maarten Baas, Einhovenseweg 104, 5582 HW Waalre, The Netherlands T. +31 (0)6 24502082 E. mail@maartenbaas.com W. www.maartenbaas.com

Page 189 ECAL (Ecole cantonale d'art de Lausanne), Département design industriel, 4 Avenue de l'Elysée, 1006 Lausanne, Switzerland T. +41 (0)21 3169220 F. +41 (0)21 3169266 W. www.ecal.ch

Page 190 Davin Wheels, 220 West Exchange Street, Suite 107, Providence, RI 02903, USA F. +1 401 2730147 E. wheelinfo@davinwheels.com W. www.davinwheels.com

Page 191 Studio Tord Boontje, *see* pages 76–7

Page 192 iiiii (Idea International), 12-6, Minami-motomachi, Shinjuku-ku, Tokyo 1 60-0012, Japan

Page 193 ClassiCon GmbH, *see* page 141

Page 194 Maharam, *see* pages 42–3

Nokia Corporation, P.O. Box 100, 00045 Finland W. www.nokia.com

Page 195 Cinal Aps, Vermundsgade 19, 2100 Copenhagen, Denmark T. +45 70226671 F. +45 70236671 E. info@cinal.dk W. www.cinal.dk

Pages 196–7 Colefax and Fowler T: +44 (0)20 8874 6484

Page 198 Dyson, Tetbury Hill, Malmesbury, Wiltshire, SN16 0RP, UK T. +44 (0)8705 275104 W. www.dyson.com

Pages 198–9 Tecno Delta srl, Via Fornace Cavallino 12/23, 20090, Opera, Milan, Italy T. +39 02 57601825 E. tecnodelta@tecnodeltaitaly.com W. www.tecnodeltaitaly.com

Page 200 Tecno Delta srl, *see* pages 198–9

Page 201 Moooi, *see* page 40

Pages 202–3 www.adidasus.com

Page 204 Design Gallery Milano, *see* pages 168–9

Pages 204–5 Maharam, *see* pages 42–3

Page 206 Bugaboo, Paasheuvelweg 29, 1105 BG Amsterdam, The Netherlands T. +31 (0)20 3119767 F. +31(0)20 6209011 W. www.bugaboo.nl

Page 207 Front, Runiusgatan 14, 11255 Stockholm, Sweden E. everyone@frontdesign.se W. www.frontdesign.se

Page 208 Front, *see* page 207

Page 209 Moooi, *see* page 40

Pages 210–1 Sawaya & Moroni SpA, Via Manzoni 11, 20121 Milan, Italy T. +39 02 86395212-218 F. +39 02 877242 E. sawaya-moroni@apm.it W. www.sawayamoroni.com

Page 212 Royal Mosa, *see* page 106

Page 213 Ineke Hans/Arnhem, *see* page 28

Page 214 Goss industrial design, Martin Buber Straße 97, 64287 Darmstadt, Germany T. +49 (0)61 519674082 F. +49 (0)61 519674083 E. info@gossindustrialdesign.de W. www.gossindustrialdesign.de

Page 215 Magis SpA, *see* page 42

ClassiCon GmbH, *see* page 141

Pages 216–7 Nike Inc, One Bowerman Drive, Beaverton, OR 97005, USA T. +1 503 671 6453 W. www.nike.com

Pages 218–9 Studio Aisslinger, Oranienplatz 4, 10999 Berlin, Germany T. +49 (0)30 31505400 F. +49 (0)30 31505401 E. studio@aisslinger.de W. www.aisslinger.de

Page 220 Flos SpA, Via Angelo Faini 2, 25073 Bovezzo (Brescia), Italy T. +39 030 24381 F. +39 030 2438250 E. info@flos.it W. www.flos.com

Page 221 Alias SpA, Via Dei Videtti 2, 24064 Grumello del Monte (BG), Italy T. +39 035 4422511 F. +39 035 4422590 E. info@aliasdesign.it W. www.aliasdesign.it

Page 222 Alias SpA, *see* page 221

Page 223 Kenwood Ltd, New Lane, Havant P09 2NH, UK T. +44 (0)2392 476000

Pages 224–5 Vitra AG *see* pages 138–9

Page 226 Kartell SpA, *see* page 50

Page 227 Covo srl, Via Degli Olmetti 3/b, 00060 Formello, Rome, Italy T. +39 06 90400311 F. +39 06 90409175 E. mail@covo.it W. www.covo.it

Pages 228–9 Cassina SpA, *see* pages 130–1

The Designs
Mikkel Adsbøl (197)
Aide à Projet VIA 2004 © Fillioux & Fillioux (113)
Akira (27)
Umberto Almiraglio (134–5)
Ramesh Amruth (164)
Artemide (57)
© Barber Osgerby (62–3, 148–9)
Gunther Binsack (103)
Duilio Bitetto (172–3)
Courtesy Bozart (29)
Santi Caleca (128)
Franco Chimenti (26)
Sergio Chimenti (18, top and 19)
Coro (165)
© Davin Wheels (192)
Mario Di Biasi (18, bottom)
Pierre Fantys/ECAL (191)
Chicco Ferretti (86–7)
Flos SpA (222)
Courtesy For the dogs (82–3)
Fotostudio Lang (90)
Julio Garcia (65)
Patrick Gries (136)
Walter Gumiero (127, 182–3, 184)
Robert Hakalski (48)
Marcus Hanschen (140, 169)
Michael Harvey (76)
Lieven Herreman (83)
Erik and Petra Hesmerg (162–3)
Peter Hill (20)
Takahiro Inoue and Studio Harada (135)
Steffen Jänicke (42, 220–1)
Magnus Klitten (34–5)
Walter Knoll (96)
John Lassen (204–5)
Holger Lübbe (216)
Carme Masià (142)
Raymond Meier (180)
Mierswa & Kluska (46)
Daniele Oberrauch (44–5)
Erwin Olaf (177, 203, 211)
Onishi photo (66)
Neal Oshima (119, 121)
Andrea Pitari (132)
Inga Powilleit (190)
RADI Designers (117)
Joachim Richau (24, 25)
Tommaso Sartori (130–1, 228–9)
Mark Serr (133)
David Spero (21)
Anita Star (114–5)
Studio Essa (19, 134)
Enrico Suà Ummarino, © Sawaya & Moroni (212–3)
Luciano Svegliado (123, 143)
Paul Tahon (138–9)
Javier Tles, Mauricio Salinas (144)
Paolo Ulian office (36)
Tom Vack (23, 72–3)
Maarten van Houten (40)
Jose van Riele (104–5)
Hajime Watanabe (84–5)
WMF (160–1)
Gionata Xerra (37)
Miro Zagnoli (226–7)
Andrea Zani (80–1)

A Flavour of 2003/4
Daniel Adric/Courtesy the Cartier Foundation (230/1)
Courtesy The Crafts Council (231/12)
Courtesy Habitat (230/3)
Courtesy Koelnmesse (230/4)
Courtesy Martin Langfield (230/5)
Courtesy Marks and Spencer picture archive (230/6, 231/8)
Courtesy Microsoft (231/11)
Courtesy Mark Newson (231/10)
Courtesy Karim Rashid Inc. (231/9)
Courtesy Moss (230/2)
Rafael Vargas (231/7)